MRS MONEYPENNY'S CAREERS ADVICE FOR AMBITIOUS WOMEN

'This wisdom-filled guide obliterates the myth that women can "have it all". It does the invaluable service of redefining success and happiness for everyone'
ARIANNA HUFFINGTON, President and Editor-in-Chief of the Huffington Post Media Group

'Mrs Moneypenny puts my hectic life in perspective – she is funny and wise, and above all, very very busy'
SARAH BROWN, author of *Behind the Black Door*

'Equal parts provocative, hilarious and wise – this book is a timely antidote to the pervasive power of male networks. It's guaranteed to get a girl's career moving'
LYNDA GRATTON, author of *The Shift*

'Want to get ahead? Then just do what Mrs M. tells you'
MERRYN SOMERSET WEBB, Editor-in-Chief, *Moneyweek*

'Warmth and wisdom shine through this tour de force of the joys, trials and tribulations of trying to have a fulfilling career as a woman'
JAN HALL, headhunter and partner at JCA Group

'Mrs Moneypenny's advice is tough, but spot on. Aim for the top. Jettison guilt. Outsource like a madwoman. Success requires sharp heels – and a sharp mind – but if you're willing to work hard, it is there for the taking'
LAURA VANDERKAM, author of *168 Hours*

ABOUT THE AUTHORS

For twelve years MRS MONEYPENNY has been
entertaining readers of the *Financial Times* with her
views on everything from Wellington boots to waxing.
She runs her own business while juggling three children
(Cost Centres #1, #2 and #3) and a golf-obsessed
husband. She has acquired a large mortgage, several
academic degrees of varying uselessness, and a passion
for shooting innocent birds. She presents the Channel 4
series *Superscrimpers*, and the Mrs Moneypenny show
has run at the Edinburgh Fringe, off-Broadway and the
Hay Festival.

DR HEATHER McGREGOR is a leading London
headhunter. She owns and runs Taylor Bennett, the
executive search firm, and teaches at the Cass Business
School and the London Business School.

www.MrsMoneypenny.com

MRS MONEYPENNY'S CAREERS ADVICE FOR AMBITIOUS WOMEN

Mrs Moneypenny
with Heather McGregor

PORTFOLIO
PENGUIN

PORTFOLIO PENGUIN

Published by the Penguin Group
Penguin Books Ltd, 80 Strand, London WC2R ORL, England
Penguin Group (USA) Inc., 375 Hudson Street, New York, New York 10014, USA
Penguin Group (Canada), 90 Eglinton Avenue East, Suite 700, Toronto, Ontario,
Canada M4P 2Y3 (a division of Pearson Penguin Canada Inc.)
Penguin Ireland, 25 St Stephen's Green, Dublin 2, Ireland
(a division of Penguin Books Ltd)
Penguin Group (Australia), 250 Camberwell Road, Camberwell,
Victoria 3124, Australia (a division of Pearson Australia Group Pty Ltd)
Penguin Books India Pvt Ltd, 11 Community Centre,
Panchsheel Park, New Delhi – 110 017, India
Penguin Group (NZ), 67 Apollo Drive, Rosedale, Auckland 0632,
New Zealand (a division of Pearson New Zealand Ltd)
Penguin Books (South Africa) (Pty) Ltd, 24 Sturdee Avenue,
Rosebank, Johannesburg 2196, South Africa

Penguin Books Ltd, Registered Offices: 80 Strand, London WC2R ORL, England

www.penguin.com

First published 2012
002

Set in 10.8/14.934 pt Sabon LT Std
Typeset by Jouve (UK), Milton Keynes
Printed in Great Britain by Clays Ltd, St Ives plc

HARDBACK ISBN: 978–0–670–92081–5
TRADE PAPERBACK ISBN: 978–0–670–92082–2

www.greenpenguin.co.uk

Penguin Books is committed to a sustainable
future for our business, our readers and our planet.
This book is made from Forest Stewardship
Council™ certified paper.

ALWAYS LEARNING   PEARSON

There are three women whose careers I follow with interest, and who have all helped to support my career, particularly in the last year.

JANE LUNNON, a deputy head teacher, whose ambitions for the girls that she taught led her to ask me to do the presentation which grew into this book.

HELEN CONFORD, an editor, whose ambitions for her employer led her to seek me out and originally ask me to write the book.

And SUSAN LEON, a senior music industry executive, whose ambitions for her client led her to meet me – which, in turn, has helped me build the confidence of hundreds, if not thousands, of ambitious women.

Thank you, all of you.

This book is dedicated to the three of you.

CONTENTS

INTRODUCTION

If you are a woman of fifteen or fifty-one, or indeed any other age, and you know that you want to reach for the stars, this book is for you.

The only qualification is that you have to want to go places in your career. If you are happy to bump along the ocean floor of life with almost everyone else, you might be happier reading a crime thriller. But if you are a woman who wants to get ahead, to swim to the top, to breathe in the oxygen that is above the waterline – or even to get some of the way towards it – buy this and read it.

Then pass it on to someone like you.

It contains the ten key things that I think women need to know if they want to succeed. They are all the things that I wish I had known at fifteen, twenty-five – or even thirty-five. I think I have achieved a lot in life. But if I had known all this, I would have achieved so much more.

Where did I learn it?

From observation and experience.

Observation is a powerful tool, especially when it is supplemented by interrogation. In my day job I meet literally hundreds of women each year, at all different stages of their careers. When I meet an interesting, aspirational or already successful woman, I turn into a sponge.

What gets her out of bed in the morning?

How is she planning to get where she is going in life?

Who, or what, has helped her achieve her goals thus far?

If I can't ask her directly, I observe, I research, I ask other people who know her.

How did Indra Nooyi end up running PepsiCo?

How did Janet Robinson end up running the New York Times Company?

How did Fiona Reynolds end up running the National Trust in the UK – an organization with 55,000 volunteer workers that cares for, among other things, over 700 miles of our coastline?

What about women I have never met, such as Gail Kelly? How did she end up running Westpac, one of Australia's largest companies? I set to and read everything I could about Ms Kelly.

And experience. I have run a successful business for quite a while now and know, very personally, which of my actions have helped that business – and which have hindered. I write a weekly column in the *Weekend Financial Times* that is read all over the world, and women everywhere write in to give me their views on what works. More recently, I presented a TV series in the UK, which led me to meet many very successful women in the media world. There are common themes running through the career success of all these women.

This book is not just for those women who want to be running big corporations, although those will be a key part of its readership. Success for some women will mean being an entrepreneur, or a leading academic, or rising to the top of the not-for-profit world. For some, success will simply mean returning to work after an extended career break to have a family.

If you are still in school, or university, or halfway through your career, or even retired and wondering if you have left it too late to try for success, read this book and see if it inspires you. There is no specific time in your career when you will need more, or less, help and support – at every age and at every stage women do better when they have the right ideas, the right focus, and the right advice.

I hope this book will provide some or all of those things for its readers.

So, why a book for women? Surely people of both sexes need help to the top?

Because women are different. And what makes us different is the simple biological fact that we have a womb. That might sound rather obvious, but this is what it means for our careers. Because many of us will have children, and will therefore almost certainly need career breaks and possibly flexibility in our employment as we raise a family, the world's employers are inclined to view us – all of us – as being distinct from our male colleagues.

You don't plan to have an employer? You are going to start your own business?

Well, the people who you will need to fund it – bankers, investors, suppliers – will also look at women differently.

Even if you plan never to have children (or to have your baby at a weekend and go back to work on the Monday), employers' views of you will be partially or wholly affected by their experience of women having children and taking time off work. It may seem that there is nothing we can do about this – after all, I doubt genetic engineering will give men wombs in my lifetime. Indeed, we may not want to. Having and raising children can be a very rewarding experience. But there are lots of ways in which women can address this often invisible image problem, and put themselves in a position to succeed.

Moira Benigson, CEO of executive search consultancy The MBS Group, is continuously amazed to meet women leaders who, despite having a successful career, are not able to play the political game as well as men.

In twenty-five years as a headhunter, I have seen women fail to manage their progression, and therefore their promotion, by not being as proactive within their career as men. When they see their ambitions fail to materialize, they may develop a "fear of flying" and choose to stay in roles that are well below their capability rather than going for the challenge of being at the top. As leadership expert Rebecca Shambaugh puts it: "It might not always be the glass ceiling, but the sticky floor" that is partly to blame.

This 'sticky floor' is widespread. In a global survey conducted by Accenture in 2011 of 3,400 business executives, 68 per cent of the women were found to believe that it took hard work and long hours to advance in a company.

Believe me, if it were just about long hours and hard work, more of us would be up there at the top. To get to the top, women need to do all the things that men do to get there – and they have to do extra as well.

What those things are, and how to go about them, is the basis of this book.

CHAPTER 1

WHAT YOU KNOW

If you are reading this book, your first question is probably, 'What can I do to give myself the best chance of career success?'

If it isn't, I suspect it should be.

We are going to start with something that seems blindingly obvious – and yet, for some reason, it is not often the first thing that people think of. You need to make sure you have all the right qualifications and experience. This is the 'what you know', which has definitely *not* been replaced by the 'who you know'.

'What you know' – things you can demonstrate on your CV – is the basic building block of any career. Get this right before you do anything else.

I am occasionally accused of being obsessed with qualifications, and it is true that I have three degrees of varying uselessness, none of which has equipped me with any particularly relevant skills. The only thing I can remember from my undergraduate degree is a diagram about how Japan supports its rice industry; from my MBA, how to sack people; and from my PhD, how to use various online academic libraries. That's it. I don't use any of these things in my day job.

So, why did I bother?

In contrast, Mr Moneypenny, my long-suffering husband, didn't trouble higher education for long. He spent a year at the University of Sydney – where he thought he was studying for a degree in cricket, with rugby union as a subsidiary subject. When he realized that the examinations he had to sit were in neither subject, he quit and went to work for a TV station (on the back of nothing more than having watched a lot of TV). Many years later, he changed career and went to work in the wine industry (on the back of nothing more than having drunk a lot of wine – although he did then do some wine industry exams, which he uses every time we buy a bottle). And then, in 2010, he went and got a cricket coaching qualification. This took twelve weeks. He got a job teaching cricket in a school, and uses what he learned every day.

So, who needs to worry about things like degrees?

But qualifications are more than just a way of acquiring skills. They are also a way of building confidence, of positioning yourself with the outside world. And they can help you develop your network – all of which will help your career.

Julia Bowden is someone who knows the value of a qualification. In 2008 she made an important but risky decision. She left her job, remortgaged her house to borrow many thousands of pounds, and went back into full-time education. Julia already had an undergraduate degree, and had graduated with excellent grades. She was thirty, and had a well-paid job in which she could have advanced further without additional formal education.

Why did she feel the need to study again? And what were the key choices she made that we can all learn from?

In returning to school, Julia was seeking to invest in – and thus increase – her stock of human capital. Accumulating human capital is the first, and most essential, part of any successful career. Human capital, like any other source of capital, is a resource that you make available to your employer (or to yourself, if you are running your own business). Your skills, experience and, crucially, qualifications are all part of your human capital.

Qualifications are indeed crucial. We can all point to successful women who have no more than a secretarial qualification – and sometimes not even that – but I promise you they are the exception. If you are ambitious, if you want to try for a highly successful and progressive career, first and foremost you need to make sure that you have the most basic requirement of all – some appropriate qualifications.

The world in which women compete for the top jobs is a brutal one. Men, of course, have known this for ever. Even an undergraduate degree is no longer the passport it once was. When I graduated from university in the UK in 1980, 18 per cent of my age group completed undergraduate degrees at a university. Now, thanks to government initiatives and the reclassification of many learning establishments as universities, it is closer to 45 per cent.

An undergraduate degree on its own is a diminished qualification. What matters more is where you studied for it, and what grade you achieved.

The good news if you are a fourteen-year-old girl reading this book, or if you know some fourteen-year-olds, is that you really can get ahead by getting good grades. In the UK we sit public exams at sixteen, exams that we start studying for at fourteen. The results are listed on our university application form and affect, just as much as our exam results at eighteen, the university place we are likely to be offered. The quality of the university where we study as an undergraduate – something that is likely to influence our entire career – is therefore affected by decisions made at the ages of fourteen, fifteen and sixteen.

And this is not just the case in the UK. College admissions in the USA are heavily influenced by PSATs, SATs and entire high school transcripts. All over the world, entrance to the more desirable places of further and higher education is determined by the grades that you achieved and the choices that you made almost before you were old enough to think about going to college.

Does that mean that if you didn't get good grades at sixteen, you should put this book down and lower your sights?

Absolutely not.

Just go on and get some good grades in the future. You can (almost) wipe out the past by investing in the future. As the late Elizabeth Taylor, herself a very ambitious woman, famously once said, 'Success is a great deodorant. It takes away all your past smells.'

You may at this point be thinking that I am only talking about MBA programmes, or other fancy postgraduate degrees. I'm not. Julia, for instance, didn't quit her full-time job to do an MBA. She studied to be a professional make-up artist.

Does this surprise you? Why did she need to do a professional qualification just to apply make-up? After all, Julia had been interested in make-up since she was a little girl, was good at doing make-up, and was frequently asked by her girlfriends to help them out on special occasions. In the world of make-up artists, as in many others, the most important reason people hire you is because you are good at your job. And you advertise that by showing your work – your portfolio – which is usually displayed on a website.

So, why not just invest in some professional photography and build a website?

Whatever that cost, it would be less than the £18,000 currently charged to complete the course that Julia studied.

While you don't need a qualification to be a successful make-up artist, you also don't need an MBA to be a successful manager. You may be amazed to know that you don't need a pilot's licence to be able to fly an aeroplane solo. Sure, in some professions – medicine, the law – you need professional qualifications to be allowed to practise, but the vast majority of people in senior positions who are running businesses around the world (me included) do not need their qualifications in order to do their job.

But – and this is the important point – they needed them to get there.

Qualifications matter. And here's why:

- they give you confidence
- they act as an independent testimony to your capability, and
- they provide you with important links to others.

Using qualifications to boost your confidence

First of all, qualifications give you confidence. Julia – you might be sick of Julia by now (the poor girl didn't even realize she was going to be in this book, she thought she was just sticking yet another set of false eyelashes on me for my TV show) – trained at Greasepaint, which is arguably one of the most famous make-up schools in the UK, and she chose it carefully. Many of the tutors at Greasepaint worked at the BBC in the days when they had an in-house make-up department and have won scores of awards for their work. Julia knew that if she trained under their supervision, she would be learning from experienced professionals, and that in itself would give her confidence when she graduated and set up as a self-employed make-up artist.

As a manager, you may never have to use half of the stuff that you learn at business school. I left business school twenty years ago, and the only technical skill that I was taught there which I have used since is how to dismiss employees. But familiarity with all the terminology and the ideas of the various disciplines taught on an MBA – from accounting and finance to change management and operational processes – made me feel much more confident as I came across these things in the workplace, and in discussion with other, more senior managers.

Confidence is a crucial attribute for a successful career. If you have studied hard, mastered what you have been taught, and have a qualification to show for your hard work, you will feel a lot more confident.

Is Julia much better, technically, at doing make-up than she was before she trained?

Yes, although she is arguably no more creative than she was before.

How much better? One hundred per cent?

Probably – not least because her course included special effects and other highly technical training.

But how much more confident is she when putting make-up on someone's face?

More like 500 per cent. That confidence comes from being taught by really experienced people and, under their supervision, putting make-up on people over and over again. And then getting excellent marks in her exams.

Confidence is an attribute that all ambitious women need to develop. The Institute of Leadership & Management (ILM) surveyed 3,000 male and female senior managers and published its findings in 'Ambition and Gender at Work' in February 2011. The confidence gap was stark: just half of the female managers described themselves as having 'high' or 'quite high' levels of confidence, compared to 70 per cent of the men. Half of the women managers admitted to feelings of self-doubt, compared to 31 per cent of the men. And 20 per cent of the men said they would apply for a role despite only partially meeting its job description, compared to 14 per cent of the women.

I am unsurprised by this. We all know that men are so much better at their own PR – not always with justification.

This gender difference in the approach to job applications is supported by Rosaleen Blair, the focused, professional but sassy and hugely likeable woman who started and runs Alexander Mann Solutions, a company that provides outsourced recruitment services.

❝ I think women are a lot less confident and a lot more self-critical than men. When applying for jobs, for example, men will tend to look at the job description and say to themselves, "I have three of the things they are looking for, so it will be fine." Whereas women might have six or seven of the same things, but because they have not got one of them they are afraid to go for it. ❞

She is not the only one who thinks this. Liz Field, CEO of the Financial Skills Partnership, says:

❝ When it comes to looking at top jobs, women are far more likely to rule out jobs even if they have little or no experience in only some aspects. That could be a lack of confidence or realism, but generally men will go for the top job regardless of whether they have all the relevant experience. ❞

Qualifications are a major source of confidence.

Think about it – do you enjoy wine? Have you become an amateur expert over the years? Do you find that you understand wine lists in restaurants so much better than your fellow diners?

Now, imagine that you had studied for and obtained a Master of Wine (MW), an international professional qualification held by fewer than 300 people, or even the Diploma in Wine, an international qualification run by the Wine & Spirit Education Trust.

Would it make you technically more able to taste and appreciate wine?

Almost certainly.

Would it make you more confident?

Definitely.

Using qualifications as an independent testimony to your capability

Secondly, and most importantly, qualifications (and/or the place you studied for them) act as independent testimony to your abilities. I am fortunate to have several Girlfriends, who readers of my column have come to know over the years by their acronyms. Examples include my Most Glamorous Girlfriend, my Most Successful Girlfriend, my Most Tenacious Girlfriend, my Investment Banker Girlfriend, my Pilates-Loving Girlfriend, and so on. Among them I have a Medical Girlfriend, Amanda Northridge, a successful doctor with her own thriving practice in the university town of Oxford.

Medical Girlfriends are very useful to have, and I commend you all to go out and get one if you haven't already. They are just the trick when your middle child (in my case, Cost Centre #2 – they are all so expensive, I have given up calling them by their real names) comes home from rowing camp with impetigo on the day Prince William marries Kate Middleton and the local surgery is closed.

Amanda is a Member of the Royal College of General Practitioners, having done the required three-year training and passed the relevant professional postgraduate examinations (after having qualified as a doctor). But she practises only private medicine – and in the UK it is not necessary to have the MRCGP qualification to practise privately as a GP.

So, why did she bother?

For one, it increased her options (she could practise in the National Health Service if she wished). But most importantly of all, it makes a statement about her that only takes five capital letters to say. And those five capital letters trumpet that Dr Northridge is as qualified in general practice as any GP working in the UK today.

You may be familiar with the argument that goes along the lines of, 'I am good at [insert skill/area of expertise] . . . I don't need a piece of paper to prove it.' I would argue that you do. If you are ambitious and want to get ahead, you need to stand out from the crowd. Suitable letters after your name, an impressive degree on your CV, or a professional qualification from a well-known institution – all these help to set you apart.

Being good at your job, in today's fiercely competitive world, is simply not enough.

Your CV is your own personal balance sheet. If you review a company's accounts, and see that they have a strong balance sheet, you are more likely to invest in that company than if they have a weak one. This is because they are more likely to be able to weather any unforeseen challenges, and also take advantage of any opportunities. They will have accumulated that balance sheet by choosing to invest in their own company rather than pay out money as dividends or salaries.

The same is true for skills and experience. If you are ambitious, making the decision to invest in yourself is never wasted.

As in the company analogy, investment is a choice. As any economics student knows, capital is a scarce resource. If you are studying for exams, or learning a new skill, you are doing that with your time, instead of spending it elsewhere.

Are you prepared to make that commitment, that choice?

If you are truly ambitious, the answer will be yes.

Let's return to the lovely Julia Bowden. (Yes! I haven't finished with her yet – the poor girl will be asking for overtime.) She invested her scarce resources – time and money – in qualifying as a professional make-up artist. Her choice of college was just as important as her decision to get a formal qualification. She chose to study at a college which is widely recognized as one of the best in the industry. She only has to mention to a producer, to another make-up artist considering subcontracting to her, or even to a potential private client that she trained at Greasepaint, and they immediately know that her work is likely to be of a specific quality.

Similarly, think what an undergraduate degree from Oxford or Cambridge, an MBA from Harvard, or the letters QC after a name all say about someone. They say straight away that this person is different, is a cut above the rest, and is in the top echelon of people in the working world. And that is before they have even opened their mouth at an interview.

Qualifications – and where you obtained them – act as a critical, unseen but hugely influential testimony for ambitious people.

So, what qualifications should you get?

Personally I would commend a qualification that is

readily understood and acknowledged by people in the world in which you want to succeed. If that is corporate life, I would aim for an accountancy or a legal qualification. (In Chapter 7 I explain why financial literacy is such an important prerequisite for successful careers.)

One qualification that I like a lot on people's CVs is the Chartered Financial Analyst (CFA). You can study for it at any time in your career, and you don't even have to attend class to do so as you can just order the books and study at home.

Are you at college? Want to get into an investment bank or a hedge fund one day?

Think how great this would look on your CV. Give up your evenings and study for it!

The CFA examinations cover the same syllabus wherever you take them and are administered by one global organization, the CFA Institute. This is a not-for-profit organization comprising the world's largest association of investment professionals. It has over 100,000 members around the world, and many more who have taken only one or two parts of what is a three-part examination.

I am sure the Institute won't thank me for this, but I often compare it with McDonald's. If you go into a McDonald's in any part of the world and order a Big Mac, what you are served will be almost identical whether you are in Shanghai, Seattle, Sydney or Singapore. The risk associated with making a decision to buy a Big Mac, or indeed any other global brand – think Pampers nappies, or PricewaterhouseCoopers accountancy services – is negligible. You know that wherever you consume their product, it will offer the same experience.

And so it is with the CFA.

There are many other qualifications that are truly international, such as studying to be a Master of Wine, as I mentioned earlier. There are currently 289 Masters of Wine in the world, based in 23 different countries, of whom 79 are women. The exam has always been open to men and women; of the 81 new Masters of Wine in the past decade, 33 are women.

Another qualification that travels well is Teaching English as a Foreign Language (TEFL).

Although they are not totally transferable to every country, qualifications in areas such as medicine, law, teaching and other professional disciplines are always useful. But even if they don't give you letters after your name, there are skills worth studying for because they will make you more employable – for example, languages or computer programming.

What about an MBA? Should you go and get one of those?

I have one, as I mentioned earlier. I remember my first day at work in Japan when my boss informed me that he, too, was an MBA – in his case this meant Married But Available.

Seriously, there is no universally applicable answer to this question – it will depend on you. Many ambitious women (me included) have found them very useful. But it is not for everyone. Hopefully this book will help you to decide if you would like to study for one – and, if you do, what to remember when deciding where to do it.

In 1986 Gail Kelly was living in South Africa, working in a bank, and was expecting her first child. Gail had taught Latin in high school when she first graduated and then moved into banking, at the South African bank Nedcor, in the 1980s, working as a teller behind the counter, because she thought there was greater opportunity in the financial services sector than in education. Spotted by her superiors as having a lot of potential, she was moved into the bank's accelerated development programme and by 1986 had risen to a mid-level position in the human resources department.

Gail, in an interview for Melbourne Business School's website, takes up the story herself. She says she realized that:

> If I intended to be serious about commerce and gaining a more senior position within financial services, I would need formal qualifications in business. I considered an accounting degree, but elected to do an MBA because of the broadening, leadership and management skills that you gain.

A job and pregnancy combined did not put her off – any more than it did me, or many other women. She did better than me, though, graduating with a distinction. (She also did better than me in producing a daughter – how come I have all sons? And for that matter, how come I am not the CEO of one of the world's largest banks? I put it all down to the fact that I didn't get a distinction in my MBA.)

What did Gail get from her MBA?

She got some skills and knowledge that were previously not even in her vocabulary. Also, it gave her confidence, and connections.

❝ It opened my thinking to the crucial areas of accounting, finance, marketing and operations management – knowledge domains that I previously had no depth in, apart from some practical exposure in the workplace. There is no question that my MBA also gave me confidence and courage to tackle the opportunities coming my way. The networks and friendships established remain current today. ❞

It is tempting to think of an MBA as a passport to better pay. GMAC, the international not-for-profit association of business schools, reported that 93 per cent of respondents from its 2010 poll in the USA were employed and had an average salary of $94,542, with a bonus of $17,565.

The other reason that some people do an MBA is to make themselves more employable. According to the London Business School, 91 per cent of the class of 2010 found jobs within three months of graduating (10 per cent up on 2009), and the average starting salary was just over £65,500. Manchester Business School's equivalent figures are 90 per cent and £55,000.

I would argue that if you are doing an MBA simply to improve your chances of getting a better job and more pay, it does not justify the huge investment of both time and money. As Tonya Olpin, executive director at the National Association of Women MBAs says, an MBA 'doesn't guarantee you a job, it gives you a toolbox. It opens up a lot of opportunities.'

She is so right.

An MBA is not an instant passport to employment, or money. Even organizations that I admire, such as the

Forté Foundation (a consortium of major corporations and top business schools that seeks 'to increase the number of women business leaders by increasing the flow of women into key educational gateways and business networks') aren't encouraging prospective students to see the value of an MBA and seem to have rather missed the point.

They set out the following reasons for doing an MBA:

- increase your earning potential
- advance within your current industry
- change your career
- gain a network of peers, faculty and alumni
- make an impact in your community.

I would say only one line of that – the network – is really important. The rest can all be achieved without an MBA.

Like any qualification, doing an MBA will bring you confidence, connections and a statement on your CV. It may well be that these, in turn, will help you get a job and/or better pay, but they are harder to achieve without capitalizing on the real benefits of an MBA. The truth is that an MBA is a general management qualification. If you want to manage a business, or even a part of one, it is very useful. End of story. If your ambition is to be the best molecular biologist in the world, or the greatest actuary, or any other technical ambition, it is totally unnecessary.

So, define your ambition, and then see if an MBA really will help you achieve it.

If you have ambitions to run a business, large or small, an MBA is probably a good idea. Anything else –

employability, higher pay – may be side benefits. But if they are the only reasons for doing an MBA, don't bother.

Evidence suggests that women are better at finding reasons *not* to do an MBA than to do one. According to the Association of MBAs, male students outnumbered female students by 70 per cent in 2010. In the UK, 53 per cent of undergraduates are female, but the percentage drops to around 30 per cent of MBA students. That is not surprising, when you consider that the best business schools require several years' experience in the workplace before admitting students.

That means that the ideal time to do an MBA is just when many women are thinking about having a baby. Mori Taheripour, Outreach Coordinator at The Wharton School of the University of Pennsylvania, put it very well.

❝ [We must] be able to show women that even though they have all of these other commitments in their lives, this is something that others can do, and others have done it. We ask for about ten years' work experience, so the average age of our students is thirty-five, and that's a point in their life where most of them have families and have senior-level positions or are entrepreneurs. So it's a challenge to get them to say, "I can add one more thing to my plate." ❞

It is possible to do an MBA and have a family at the same time. I did it. Gail Kelly did it. And lots of women have done (or are doing) it.

My friend Henrietta Royle, champion of women in the boardroom and someone with boundless energy, is a former chief operating officer of CASS Business School in London. She has seen dozens of women with families complete not just MBAs but many other master's programmes. In an interview with *The Independent* newspaper in the UK in April 2011, Henrietta expressed what many of us know (a view that the paper described as 'pragmatic'): 'If you want to do it, you'll get organized. There's no reason that you can't do it because of children, especially when the trade-offs can be so great in later life'.

Business schools are sympathetic to mothers studying for MBAs. My own experience was that when it all became too much for me after the birth of my first son, they let me drop a year before carrying on. It meant starting again with a new study group, but that was so much better than giving up altogether – or never starting in the first place.

More than two decades later, things have really moved on. The University of Indianapolis, for example, offers a Saturday-only option, and offers expectant mothers the option to take a semester off for maternity leave.

Rachel Killian, a mother of two who was recently studying on the Warwick Business School Executive MBA programme (a two-year part-time course), while continuing to work in the school's marketing department, explains how she managed.

❛ It's all about balance. People need to choose a programme and a school that fits their life. I'll go home, spend a few hours with the kids, then when they've gone to bed I'll get my books out instead of sitting in front of the TV. Everyone's different. But the rewards will be much greater than the compromises. ❜

It is about priorities more than about balance. If you are an ambitious woman who feels that an MBA is for her, you will make the time – even if you are expecting a family. Something else will be removed – TV watching, in Rachel's case – to make room for it. Do you really need to watch *Footballers' Wives*, or another episode of *Keeping Up with the Kardashians*? Surely you can record them? Dust on the shelves won't kill you. You don't need to iron everything; you don't have to buy and read *Hello!* magazine; that novel you like the idea of will wait a few more months.

In fact, it is hard to think of any reason at all why you couldn't find time to do an MBA – if you really want to.

Using qualifications to forge important links to others

If you have decided to do an MBA – and got rid of the excuse that you are too busy because you have, or are expecting to have, a family – where should you apply?

Apply to an accredited school. Apply to one that is well up – or rising fast – in the league tables. Remember why you are going – the teaching is only part of it. The reputation benefits and the networking opportunities that come with an MBA (or, indeed, any qualification) from a good school mean that you should attend the most prestigious school you can get into or reasonably attend. I would argue that it is almost better to have no MBA than one from a substandard school – especially when you consider the time and money that you will have to invest.

The better the school, the greater the connections they will give you.

Take advantage of the gender imbalance – there are scholarships available to women to study for an MBA across Europe and in the USA. The London Business School, Leeds University Business School, the European School of Management and Technology in Berlin, IMD Business School in Switzerland and The Wharton School of the University of Pennsylvania all offer scholarships to women. Or you can apply for a fellowship through a foundation, such as the Forté Foundation. Forté offers scholarships at any one of 39 participating schools in Europe, the USA, Asia and Australia and you can be of any nationality. There is also the McCallum Leadership Scholar Program at Bentley University (Boston), for applicants from minorities.

It doesn't matter what qualification you pursue, how well it is regarded by present and future employers will largely depend on the reputation and track record of where you studied for it. The CFA might be organized on a global scale and supported by a huge marketing budget, but for less-specific qualifications, such as an MBA (or even an undergraduate degree), the place where you studied and the grade that you achieved are more important than the qualification itself.

Yes, I know it seems unfair, but we all know the world isn't fair. Anyone over the age of seven who uses the word 'unfair' has a very loose grasp on reality.

An MBA from Harvard is more prestigious than an MBA from the University of Stirling, though both have well-regarded teachers.

Is that because the curriculum at Harvard differs from Stirling?

No. It is because the Harvard brand is more prestigious.

How has that happened? Have Harvard hired better marketing people?

They may well have done. But, if they have, it is because they can afford a better marketing team than Stirling. In fact, they can afford better everything than Stirling – better faculty, better buildings, better marketing, and more financial assistance for students, meaning they can attract some of the brightest and best applicants in the world.

Why is this?

To find the answer, we need to look just to the southwest of London Bridge. Here sits, incongruously amid a major road-traffic crossing of the Thames and one of the busiest train termini in the city, and adjacent to a well-known food market, the cathedral church of the diocese of Southwark. It was here that John Harvard, born a butcher's son in London in 1607 before emigrating to the USA, was baptized. The relevant entry, with his father's signature, is in the cathedral register. The cathedral is open to visitors free of charge, and it has a side chapel dedicated to John Harvard, the restoration of which was paid for by Harvard alumni.

It should be a place of pilgrimage for all ambitious women – not just for the peace and quiet it affords to allow contemplation of the struggle ahead, but also for what it tells us about Harvard as an institution and why it is successful.

What strikes any visitor familiar with university development programmes is how long ago the chapel was restored. The splendid stained-glass window was donated by Harvard graduate and then US Ambassador to London, Joseph Hodges Choate. He was present at its official unveiling on 22 May 1905. The window depicts the baptism of Christ and the arms of Emmanuel College Cambridge, which John Harvard attended (itself pretty good on any CV), as well as Harvard University.

I sat in that chapel one day – not to worry about the struggle ahead, but because I was early for a meeting at the *Financial Times* – and thought about what I could learn from the chapel. I decided that the major lesson was that Harvard Business School is a powerful and influential brand on your CV because its alumni keep it that way – just as they keep the chapel looking good.

Business schools, universities and even high schools try to encourage alumni to stay in touch, to support the establishment where they studied. As far as I can see, they do so for the most part by appealing to the alumni's sense of altruism – we gave you a good education, now it is your turn to give us something. But I believe that is a flawed argument – for two reasons.

First, a degree – especially a postgraduate degree, if you have paid for it all yourself (and most people do) – is a commercial transaction. I pay you, and you educate me. We both fulfil our side of the bargain and then we go our separate ways. Any attempt to call on affection I may have for the place (which works well, especially when an institution appeals to people's ego and pride) is a kind of emotional blackmail; there is no contractual –

written or unwritten – obligation on me to support the place after I leave.

The second reason, which is by far the more important one, is this: your qualification will be on your CV – your personal balance sheet – for the rest of your life. The institution which awarded it to you will be a brand that you are associated with for ever. That's fine while it is one of the leading educational establishments in the world, but what happens once it falls into decline? It is your CV it will be sitting on.

Can you afford, for your own sake and the sake of your career, not to support it?

Harvard alumni, whether they realize it or not, have a contractual obligation to themselves to support their Alma Mater. If they do, the Harvard Business School, and Harvard itself, will continue to be able to afford great buildings, the best teachers, and to financially support the world's best students, as well as hiring the best marketing and development staff. This, in turn, will maintain Harvard's world reputation, and keep the brand looking strong on the CVs of its graduates.

Mr Choate knew that back in 1905.

And it remains true for every university, business school and even high school. The greater its achievements, the more influence it will have on the ambitions of its alumni.

Not all of us – indeed, not even most of us – will be able to contribute vast quantities of cash to an endowment. What if you have just graduated and have no money? You're certainly in no position to enjoy a building named after you, after writing a cheque with six or seven zeroes after the first digit. You're too busy writing cheques to the bank that loaned you the money to pay for your studies. But even $10 a year is worth having – remember how many students a college or university has.

You need to invest in your college because it is important for your CV, as well as for secondary things such as your network. So, even if you are at the very start of your career, remember that you have assets other than money – you have time. And that time could be used interviewing applicants, speaking at open days, writing for websites about your experiences as a student and why you would recommend that people follow in your footsteps. All of these activities are just as valuable as cash, although institutions do need both. In fact, in the USA, making a financial contribution, however small, helps to increase a university's score in the league tables, because the percentage of alumni who contribute is measured and the university ranked accordingly.

When I graduated from the London Business School twenty years ago, it wasn't that well regarded internationally. I had negative earnings because I also had a young child, and the childcare was expensive. But I gave my time to the school and interviewed for them, spoke at open days wherever in the world I was subsequently based, and, ever since I have been able to do, have supported them financially in a modest but consistent way. During that time, they have risen from being a prominent business school to being, by some measures, the best international business school in the world. I do not flatter myself that I am responsible – my efforts are but a rounding error compared to those of thousands of others. But I do believe that if everyone who ever studied at the London Business School contributed even as modest an amount of money and time as I have, it will remain in the premier division for my – and their – working lifetime.

That will maintain the value of the asset of having studied there.

As my MBA cost a lot of money, which I had to borrow and repay, it makes a lot of sense to keep that value current.

If your school is currently in the second tier, think what can be achieved through collective action.

Adding the right experience to your qualifications

Having stressed the importance of qualifications, they are almost totally useless without relevant experience.

Getting relevant experience in the industry in which you wish to work can be tough – sometimes it means starting again at the bottom. Gail Kelly was an accomplished and experienced high school teacher and gave it up to work behind the counter at a bank. Now she is ranked as the eighth most powerful woman in the business world.

Another former school teacher who I like and admire tremendously is Janet Robinson, CEO of the New York Times Company. Janet used to teach in a school in Massachusetts but, like Gail Kelly, thought that education would be a limiting career. So, she came to New York city looking for a job. She was a good tennis player and got herself a job selling advertising space at *TENNIS* magazine. The rest, as they say, is history. When Janet invited me for lunch in the NYT building overlooking the Hudson, and took me to see the wall of photos of people working there who have won the Pulitzer Prize, I realized just how inspirational her story was. She had been a qualified teacher with ten years' experience. And yet, to achieve her ambitions, she started all over again flogging ad space in a magazine.

Just getting a foot in the door, like Gail and Janet, can take lateral thinking and careful planning. My friend Helen Weir joined Unilever's graduate training scheme when she graduated from Oxford, then studied for an MBA at Stanford before joining McKinsey. After she had been at McKinsey for some years, she wanted to move into corporate life, and worked out how she was going to do it. When she had been at Unilever, she had (like all the people on their graduate scheme) studied for her management accountancy exams and so, although she had not used them for years, she made the most of having a financial qualification and got a job as the financial controller of a division of a large retail group. Eventually, she became the finance director of the whole place, and was catapulted firmly into the spotlight. Many years and a few different roles later, she was appointed a non-executive director of SABMiller, one of the world's largest drinks companies.

Experience, when added to qualifications, is very powerful when you are competing for the top jobs. But getting the right experience, however well qualified you are, can be challenging.

Think laterally when you are trying to break into a new area. Whether it is your tennis skills, or that management accountancy qualification that you had almost forgotten you had, women who succeed are working out what they have that others might want – even if it is not the most obvious thing on their CV.

The other winning strategy when trying to gain experience in a new industry is to apply to a part of the company that no one wants to work in, or would think of working in. Getting in the door is the biggest challenge – if you are any good, you will be able to move around once you arrive. I counsel people wanting to get into investment banking to apply to internal audit, finance or even human resources. And I advise people who want to break into TV to start in advertising sales or the legal department.

When I obtained my MBA in 1992, the UK was in the depths of a recession. But I wanted a job in a securities company, selling UK equities to fund managers. I planned my assault on London's stockbrokers meticulously. I had been working for a company where part of my role involved dealing with its shareholders. Our biggest shareholder was then the fund management arm of the insurance company Scottish Widows. I asked the fund manager we dealt with there for the names of the stockbrokers to whom they handed most of their orders. He named four. So, I wrote to all four, having carefully researched the name of the person heading the equity sales desk. I mentioned that I knew one of his – and all four were a 'he' – clients, and was keen to work in equity sales.

I got three interviews and two job offers.

Relevant experience is important, and it is better to have that experience without a break.

Why?

Because it is really difficult to get back into work after a break. Whole books have been devoted to the subject. A break can also erode your confidence, and make you less attractive to employers because you are less current. So, if you are planning a career break – to have a family, or just because you want to sail around the world – think about how it is going to look on your CV. With the right planning, there is nothing wrong with a career break – even for the most ambitious woman.

Personally, I didn't really do maternity leave. When my first Cost Centre was born, I gave the whole nappies/sleepless nights gig a two-week run and then fled back to the office, having hired the maternity nurse equivalent of a Rolls-Royce – a Norland Nanny.

It took five years before I could be persuaded to have another go, and the timing went wrong when Cost Centre #2 arrived four weeks early and right in the middle of a deal I was working on. In hospital I had fabulous care for me and him, and so could work uninterrupted. But then, disaster – my medical insurance only covered me to be in hospital for a week. So, much to Mr M.'s horror, I refused to go home with my new baby and checked into the Berkeley Hotel, where I spent another week writing the prospectus while the hotel staff rallied round. (They even found non-biological washing powder for his laundry, and a nanny to walk him round Hyde Park each day.) By the time CC#3 showed up, four years later, email and the Internet had arrived, and working from my hospital bed was easy.

But I am not a good example, or even anything approaching 'normal'. Most women will want a career break when they have a family, even if it is only a few months. If you are among them, and plan to return to your career – or even have the option to do so – you need to think about how to keep your CV current.

A few years ago, I advised a young woman who could not stay in her senior role (on account of child number three's arrival) on how to bridge the gap until she could resume full-time work. I suggested that she work during her career break, but in a totally different job – that she take up teaching finance, instead of doing it. The plan succeeded – she is now a senior financial manager at a telecommunications company.

I asked her recently how she had felt about this at the time I gave her the advice. Her response was illuminating.

I had never considered being a teacher – I thought "no way"! But teaching finance and investor relations turned out to be a fantastic job in so many ways. It was part-time, so fitted around childcare responsibilities, but didn't have the stigma that part-time jobs can have. It gave me the opportunity to work in a smaller entrepreneurial environment, which is very positively viewed by many people who I work with now. Most importantly, from a career point of view, it enabled me to stay current with financial market regulations in a way that meant I was more up to speed than when I had been working in the corporate market. Training also afforded me insight into companies other than the one I had been with all my working life, and different departments, such as corporate communications.

Another friend whose career break was an excellent example of how to stay current was Anne Spackman, now the comment editor of *The Times*. She had been a successful young news journalist, and was part of the team that launched *The Independent*. But when she had her sons, she decided to find a role that would keep her in journalism but with very limited hours. She resigned as weekend editor of *The Independent* and offered to be the property correspondent for a salary that was the equivalent of the budget for the property page. That meant writing two pieces a week (at any time of any day) rather than working a set number of days. She worked an average of twenty-seven hours a week.

Why did she choose this route?

Not every ambitious journalist, and especially not one who had Anne's achievements on their CV, would want to write about four-bedroom semi-detached houses and mortgage interest rates. But she realized that by doing this (rather than stopping altogether) it would at least keep her in touch with the newspaper and earning some money, while allowing her time with her young family. She recalled in a recent conversation with me that she embraced her new career with enthusiasm.

I thought papers failed to reflect how important property was as a subject for their readers – this was in the days before property sections. It gave me a chance to write on everything from the economics of interest rates to the lives of the rich and famous in a field where few journalists were competing. I loved it.

Anne was then headhunted by the *Financial Times* to do their property coverage, which added further to her CV. When her children were older, she moved back into full-time work when she was headhunted by *The Times* to launch their stand-alone property insert. It has been a great commercial success. She was subsequently appointed to run the project to move *The Times* into tabloid format, then became managing editor, then editor-in-chief of *Times Online*, and now comment editor.

The net result of all of this is that her husband, who was the main breadwinner through all the years of childrearing and writing about property, is now able to pursue his own highly successful plural career.

What have we learned in this chapter?

Qualifications are important, because they boost confidence, act as independent testimony to your capabilities, and provide links to other people.

Where you study for them matters almost as much as what qualification you get. This is a major reason to support the places of learning that you have been part of, and which will always be on your CV.

Experience is important too, and you should think laterally about how to get experience with relevant places.

Plus, we have learned that Julia Bowden is an excellent example! (And perhaps *she* should learn not to share so much with people when she is putting their eyeliner on. They might be writing a book in their spare time.)

So, what you know is necessary. But, as students of logic know, necessary does not always mean sufficient. To be really successful, you need to combine 'what you know' with 'who you know', which is the subject of the next chapter.

HOMEWORK FOR AMBITIOUS WOMEN

At the start of your career

1. How should you decide if you are studying the right subjects? Look at what you hope to do next, find people who work or teach there, and ask them.
2. How can you get the experience that you need for the future? Write down the three companies where you would most like to intern, then explore lateral ways to work there.
3. Is there a professional qualification that you think could help your career? Work out when you might be able to study for it – no excuses.

At a more advanced stage

If your career is not where you think it should be, consider the following.

1. Is there a postgraduate qualification that you should be studying for? List the reasons why you might not be able to start studying for it during the next twelve months. How can you overcome them?
2. Contact an executive search firm or sit down with a more senior member of your profession/company and show them your CV. Ask them what extra experience or qualifications would transform it. Then set yourself a twelve-month deadline to at least get started on addressing the things they identify.

CHAPTER 2

WHO YOU KNOW

What you know represents the foundations of your career. But you won't be able to build much above the first floor if you don't have the right materials, and the most important material of all is connections – a network.

I have no time at all for people who think that life should be a meritocracy, that it should be about 'what you know' rather than 'who you know'. The truth is, if you want to achieve your goals in life, you need to be both good at what you do and good at building relationships with people who matter.

I can best illustrate this with a tale of two breakfasts.

In January 2006 Cynthia Carroll was staying, alone, in a hotel in Switzerland. She was already a successful businesswoman, being the CEO of Alcan Primary Metal Group, the second-largest producer of aluminium in the world. She had turned forty-eight just six weeks earlier. (In one account of this story that I have read, she was described as 'a middle-aged American businesswoman'. I rather object to the term 'middle-aged'. Have you met her? There is nothing at all middle-aged about Cynthia Carroll.)

Coming down to breakfast at the unholy hour of 07.00, there was only one other person in the room, a friendly white-haired Englishman. She went and sat next to him, and got chatting. His name was Sir Mark

Moody-Stuart, and he was the chairman of the mining company Anglo American, one of the biggest companies in the world. Less than ten months later, Ms Carroll was appointed as Anglo's first female, and first non-South African, CEO.

What do we learn from this?

We learn to have breakfast in Switzerland in January. If we do, we have a greater than average chance of our dreams coming true. Every January, in a small ski resort in the eastern reaches of Switzerland, the world's political and business leaders gather, together with a smattering of opinion formers from the worlds of art, science and economics, to debate the burning issues of the day. This is the Annual Meeting of the World Economic Forum (WEF) held each year in Davos.

It is no good being brilliant at running companies involved with metal if no one knows about it.

But surely Cynthia Carroll's track record at Alcan should have spoken for itself? Did she really need to show up in Switzerland and meet Sir Mark Moody-Stuart in order to get added to the shortlist by the headhunter working for Anglo?

Sir Mark Moody-Stuart is an experienced chairman with a worldwide reputation, and he would not have given someone a job on the basis of one random breakfast encounter. Ms Carroll (whose CV includes a Harvard MBA and several years running a large quoted company) would have had lots of interviews, both with the headhunter and members of the Anglo board, and would have been compared to several other candidates before being offered the job. But the world's leading headhunters, I can tell you from first-hand knowledge, are not computers, they are people. When candidates are being considered for roles, personal recommendation goes a long way. And the personal recommendation of the chairman would have gone even further.

He had met her, talked to her, been impressed by her.

Two years later, in January 2008, I was staying, alone, in a hotel in Switzerland. I was already a successful entrepreneur, and had my own weekly column in the *Weekend Financial Times*. I was six weeks shy of my forty-sixth birthday. Coming down to breakfast at a less unholy hour of 08.00, I noticed a friendly face. No, it was not Sir Mark Moody-Stuart; it was someone I had met briefly once before, the European boss of a global payment processing company. I went and sat next to him, and we got chatting.

The next day, he sent me an invitation to shoot partridge in Spain. At the time, I had never been shooting in Spain and had always longed for an invitation, not just because the weather is so much more appealing than in the UK, but because serious C-Suiters (the highest-level executives – CEOs, COOs and CFOs) and their advisers shoot there.

Sure enough, when I went, the sun shone – and my fellow guests were people of enormous value to my business who I would normally have struggled to meet.

In these days of Facebook, Twitter, LinkedIn and other social media that are able to connect millions of people, is it necessary to go to Switzerland in January, or to go shooting in Spain?

The WEF, even for those attending, can be, as one

(male) CEO said to me, 'a bit of a zoo'. The security is on a par with any major airport. Accommodation is scarce and the chances are that unless you are the President of the United States or the chairman of one of the world's largest banks, you will be billeted in Klosters, almost half an hour away by car. And if you are even more obscure than that, such as my good self, you can find yourself sleeping somewhere halfway to Zurich and having to set off before daylight to make any kind of 08.00 meeting.

So, is Davos necessary?

The answer is yes.

You may think all the debates could just be viewed via webcast. But the proliferation of social media makes face-to-face interaction even more important. Because so many people are connected through the Internet, it is difficult to distinguish between them. You need to meet lots of people, in person, before you can work out who you really want in your community, and who you are happy to leave out.

Deciding who to include in your network

I use three filters. None of them are, 'Will this person be useful to me in the future'? Not only is it impossible to tell the answer to that question (far better to assume that everyone you ever meet might have a part to play in your future, and treat them accordingly), using it as your filter would make you a selfish person who is unlikely to be able to build a network of any lasting value.

My three filters (and for a long time I didn't even know I was applying them) are these.

1. Do I like this person? Do I enjoy their company, do I feel valued by them, would I be happy if I were stuck on a train journey to Scotland with them?
2. Do I admire this person? Do I admire their achievements, their skills, or something else about them – for example, their generosity and kindness? Am I inspired by them? Do I feel I could learn from them?
3. Do I trust this person? This might be a gut instinct at first, but will ultimately be based on experience, so I usually have to meet them several times.

You don't need to fit all three of these criteria for me to want you in my network. Of course, it would be great if you did. But just one of them is enough for me to want to build a relationship with you.

Whatever filter you use, it is important to build a network. I know that many people, of both sexes, find this challenging. But women seem to find it more so than men, and, according to a recent article in the *Harvard Business Review*, fail to cultivate enough of what the author describes as 'relationship capital'. Some of us just can't find the time, and some of us don't enjoy meeting new people and find ourselves resenting the time and effort that goes into staying in touch with them.

But if you are headed for the top, of any profession, a network is not just a 'nice-to-have', it is a 'must-have'.

So, get out and meet people.

Your approach to building good connections

Here are some top pointers from a book on networking, published recently.

- Remember that we meet people all the time, so building a network doesn't just happen at 'events'. Develop a style that works for you and shows people the real 'you' – personal chemistry counts for a lot.
- A good place to start is offering help to others when you don't need anything yourself. Decide what the top two or three things are that you want people to remember you for – know what your strengths are and play to them.
- If you are out of work, have a high-quality, professional-looking business card printed.
- Never be disparaging about others – it makes others wonder what you'll say about them behind their back. And it is, after all, a small world.
- Keep a database – try and add in some ice-breaker personal details such as children's names and, if possible, when you last spoke and what about.

Also, go out to events and occasions that you might not feel like attending. This is especially true at the start of your career. You never know who you might meet.

I am occasionally accused of being prepared to go to the opening of an envelope. This is totally untrue – it depends on the size, shape and colour of the envelope. Oh, and what kind of paper it is made of. What is true is that when I first changed careers and started my own business, I went to anything and everything. Including things I was not invited to.

When I quit working in an investment bank in 2000, I discovered that I had become a nonentity overnight. Suddenly all the industry events I had previously been invited to as a matter of course, and which I now realized were full of useful contacts, never seemed to include me.

One such event was an award ceremony for small and medium-sized public companies, which was held in a swanky hotel in London. I decided to go anyway, totally uninvited. The trick I used was to turn up in an evening gown with an evening bag but no coat (it was early March, and freezing) and then enter, looking as though I had just been outside for a cigarette. This worked a treat and so I joined the pre-dinner drinks easily, going up and chatting to people I already knew and getting them to introduce me to others. None of them knew I was there uninvited.

The crunch time came when dinner was called, because I had nowhere to sit. I quickly ran my eye over the table plan and discovered that the *Financial Times* had a table. Nipping down to the dining area in advance, I asked the waiting staff to lay up an extra place on the *FT* table.

The table was hosted by the *FT*'s commercial section. Their guests were all advertisers in the paper. I got lucky – the advertisers were so delighted to meet someone from editorial that no one thought to ask exactly how I had arrived at the table. I met lots of interesting people that evening, and then followed up with letters and emails. I suggested to one of the table hosts I met that night that he should invite me the following year, which he duly did.

Over time, I have successfully crashed almost every event that matters – although I've usually managed to find a legitimate way in eventually. I won't be naming the events, or how I managed it, in case the organizers close the loopholes!

Recognizing the importance of connections

There is nothing new about the importance of connections. There is even an academic term for it – 'social capital' – which was coined almost a hundred years ago. I wrote my PhD thesis on this kind of stuff, but I won't bore you with the textbook references. The idea is that your connections are as valuable to you – and, crucially, to your present and future employers – as your qualifications and experience. So, it is very important, if you are going to reach the top, to develop a strong personal network of contacts.

A word here on abuse of the English language. I absolutely hate the use of the word 'network' as a verb. As a noun, a (social) network is defined as a 'usually informally interconnected group or association of persons (as friends or professional colleagues)'. 'Network' is not a transitive verb – at least, not when applied to the establishment of relationships. It can be used as an intransitive verb – to engage in networking can mean 'the exchange of information or services among individuals, groups, or institutions; specifically, the cultivation of productive relationships for employment or business'.

These days, people can build huge 'personal networks' in cyberspace. But I am not talking about the virtual kind. How many people you know, or even how important they are, is not nearly as crucial as how well you know them. I define someone as being part of my network if they will return my email or telephone call.

How many people is that for you?

If you ever feel that building a career seems like too much hard work and suspect you are in need of an energy transfusion, try to hear Lynda Gratton speak. Lynda is Professor of Management Practice at my Alma Mater, the London Business School, and is that great combination of being both an inspiration and an education. She is the person for whom the term 'infectious enthusiasm' was invented. Seven years older than me, Lynda looks five years younger and has the energy levels of someone ten years younger. And she is not short of ambition – she has said on the record that she wants to 'change the world'. This bubbly, glamorous mother of two, a grammar school girl brought up in Cumbria, has published scores of papers and seven books, the most recent of which is *The Shift*, in which she writes extensively on the importance of networks.

When I first heard Lynda speak about networks, she barely used the word at all. She coined a term that I think describes my own network exactly: 'a regenerative community'. Brilliant! Because that is what the best network is – a collection of relationships with people who themselves introduce new people to you. Any network – sorry, community – will have an element of natural wastage, and some of the best people to help you fill the vacancies are the ones you meet through existing connections – because they will, in effect, have been pre-screened for you.

In her latest book, Lynda says that she thinks everyone will need to have three distinct networks in order to 'create value'.

The 'Posse'

This is your first and closest network. These are the people that you can rely on to help you tackle any major challenge. It is probably a relatively small group of people, who have some of the same expertise that you have. There is enough overlap for you to really understand each other and add value quickly. Your 'Posse' trust you – they have 'ridden out' with you before – and you will have been there for them in the past.

For me, in my professional life, the Posse are my colleagues at work. I run a small company, with fewer than twenty people, but I know I could rely on each and every one of them to ride out for me if I needed them. They all know me well and have been on the frontline with me before. We have tackled tough challenges together (both professional and personal), and they know that I would ride out for them too.

At home, this would be my husband and the Cost Centres, my parents, plus a very small number of my closest girlfriends who I know would immediately jump to help me out with anything, without asking questions or making judgements.

Who does your Posse consist of?

Your 'Big Ideas' Network

The second network of the three that Lynda thinks you need to succeed is your 'Big Ideas' Network, made up of connections to people who are completely different from you. It's in the combination of their ideas and your ideas that the Big Ideas emerge, the value of which lies in keeping you thinking outside the box. She reckons that this network will include people you just happen to bump into, or who are friends of friends. They may be completely different from you, yet together you are prepared to jump across the boundary to make a connection.

There are lots of them: while your Posse could be as few as three people, your Big Ideas Network could be hundreds, even thousands. Lynda even thinks that this network may be virtual – accessed through Facebook, Twitter or reading their blogs. (I presume that Lynda does not include LinkedIn. LinkedIn has a place in the life of an ambitious woman, as we shall see later in this book, but won't help her generate Big Ideas.)

I don't have a Facebook page, I have a Twitter handle but don't tweet, and have only ever followed one person's blog – that of the *FT*'s former news editor as he flew from London to South Africa. (I did get a Big Idea from him, though, and that was to fly myself from London to South Africa.) This lack of interest in engaging with the virtual world is probably generational, but I do understand the need for a Big Ideas Network. Looking back at all my Big Ideas, both at work and at home, I can see that they were influenced by people I had met who I had almost nothing in common with.

The 'Regenerative Community'

Finally, the third network that Lynda thinks we need to succeed is the one she terms the 'Regenerative Community'. As I said, I like this title; for me, I suspect my Big Ideas Network and my Regenerative Community are one and the same – a large network of people who I am not particularly close to (or, in most cases, have much in common with) but who I respect, trust, am interested in, and whose company I enjoy. My ideas come from them – as do my inspiration and most of my new contacts – and they are invaluable when trying to achieve my goals.

Lynda explained to me, over a glass or two of Italian white wine, that she had not used the word 'regenerative' in the way that I had interpreted it. By a 'regenerative network' she means a network of people who energize you, inspire you, get you off your backside and out to get things done. I, of course, mean people who repopulate your network.

But either way, we agreed that a network was vital for ambitious women.

Janet Hanson knows about regenerative communities. A managing director at Goldman Sachs and mother of two, Janet founded 85 Broads in 1997. Janet originally built 85 Broads so that current and former women of Goldman Sachs had a network with which to share their careers and personal lives. (The address of Goldman Sachs in New York is 85 Broad Street.) The network currently has more than 20,000 members and includes professional women of diverse backgrounds. It has been a regenerative community not only for Janet, but for thousands of women around the world.

Maintaining your network of contacts

An important and obvious place to start is within the company or organization where you currently work. Internal networks afford support, inside information and the heads-up on job opportunities. These networks should include the more powerful within a company but also co-workers at all levels.

A study of more than 100 senior women in financial services in 2011 concluded that many women had come across 'unhelpful' behaviours amongst fellow women who were reluctant to help each other, because nobody had helped them. This is very short-sighted thinking. One book about female leadership reminds us that workplace advancement 'flows from supporting one's colleagues and not merely from expecting help from them'.

In other words, it's a two-way street.

And it can get quite messy. Internal politics exists in all companies, big and small, and is a reality that some women have been reluctant to be part of – to their detriment, according to Avivah Wittenberg-Cox and Alison Maitland in their useful book *Why Women Mean Business*.

When women condemn politics [in the workplace] and stay away from it, they effectively remove themselves from the game, without consciously acknowledging it. They spend all of their time on carrying out the content of their job description. Smart employers know this – and love them for it – which is why women are so appreciated in middle management. They make great worker bees. But the worker bees become frustrated when they see that the colleagues who get promoted are the ones who have spent a lot of time networking, building alliances, and 'managing up'.

If you want to get to the top, doing your job is just not enough. If you want to build your career much further than the first floor, you really do need a network.

You will also guess that I am a firm believer in persistence – it usually pays off.

Crystal Christmas-Watson, general manager of Residence Inn by Marriott Pentagon City, was an ambitious young woman who was very keen to move to a position in the sales team. She asked her boss to introduce her to the regional sales manager the next time he was in town. Crystal's story was featured on the Working Mother website.

The meeting was cordial but brief – there were no openings – but Crystal persisted. 'Every time he came by, there I was asking, "Can I have five minutes of your time?"' she recalls with a laugh. Eight months later, Crystal was accepted into the company's sales training program.

Valuing the members of your network

One of the most challenging things about building a network is that you may end up with more valuable members than hours in the day. Also, it is important that members of the community feel valued by you – as one banker said to me last year, if being a member of my community does not make someone feel special, they won't want to be part of it. (Just to remind you, I would describe someone as being 'in my community' when I know that they will definitely return a telephone call or email.)

Received wisdom says that most people cannot manage a community beyond about 1,000 people. I probably manage one of 2,500 people. The key to making sure you stay in touch is to see these people face-to-face as often as you can. Students of something called 'media richness theory' know that email and other electronic communication (including social media) are not particularly strong means of building relationships – which is not surprising when you consider that 85 per cent of communication is non-verbal.

But face-to-face is hard to achieve with so many people on a one-to-one basis, and it would be easy to burn out – especially in the early days of your career, when you're trying to build your regenerative community.

One of my longest-serving employees recently introduced me to her friend Marisa Leaf, the founder and managing director of London-based food delivery company Hubbub. Marisa, who is still in her early thirties, says that it is easy to blur the boundaries between work and the rest of your life when you run your own business – especially when the business has a social element to it, like food.

Most businesses rely on networks of one kind or another; it would be easy for me to spend every evening and weekend at food tasting events, supper clubs, cookery classes, talks, pitches, entrepreneurs, clubs and so on because they're undeniably useful – and a lot of fun. But the lack of boundaries between work and private life, and being constantly "on call" can come at a cost to your private life and your ability to think clearly.

As Marisa is finding, it is hard trying to manage a network.

How should you allocate your time so that you see enough people, but it doesn't take over your life?

Time alone, thinking time, is very valuable, as Marisa has learned.

I recommend having small gatherings on a regular basis, and even a larger one once a year or so. Even better, try and create a 'proprietary' event. There are some such events in the UK that people would almost kill for an invitation to.

One of the best examples of this is the gala preview of the Chelsea Flower Show, held on the Monday night of the show, where tickets cost upwards of £500 and are so scarce that most are allocated by ballot. Banks, accountancy firms and lawyers use this event to entertain all their most senior clients. You may wonder why so many chairmen and CEOs have an interest in flowers, let alone why they make sure their travel schedules bring them to the UK on the third Monday in May. This is because the hosts are very clever – they invite all the spouses. This has created an event that people do not dare miss.

When I bought my business, nearly seven years ago, I was mentored by the CEO of one of the world's biggest consumer goods companies, and he told me that the most important thing was to create a proprietary event.

I have tried to create several.

I hold a private breakfast once a month at the Walbrook Club – a private members' club in the heart of London's financial district – in a private room, for six to eight people. Breakfast is a good meal because it only requires busy people to give up an hour or so, not the three hours needed for dinner. I don't have a speaker, but I do ask one journalist and one banker to each breakfast, so the people coming know the other guests will be interesting. I restrict the people I invite – and guests, I hope, feel special. I keep notes of who to ask as I go along in my day-to-day work. Then, once a month, I send out invites and give people forward dates (in case they cannot do the one I am asking them to).

Another proprietary event that I have developed is a ladies' clay shooting day each spring to introduce women to the sport (and each other). In the UK, many of the most senior people in corporations, plus bankers, lawyers and accountants, have, in effect, a 'club' of people who hang out with each other and shoot birds together. There is no 'formal' club, of course – what happens is that people meet at shoots and build relationships, and then invite each other. I know of one CEO who, when he was appointed, was taken aside by his chairman and instructed to learn to shoot, in the interests of developing the connections he would need in order to be an effective CEO.

There are very few women in this corporate 'club'. But shooting is actually a good sport to take up as a woman, because (unlike tennis or golf, for instance) women can compete on a level playing field. If you are bad at golf, you can seriously hamper your playing companions' enjoyment of the day. In shooting, if you are not very good (and I am really very average), it won't affect anyone else you are shooting with – unless, of course, you shoot them, Dick Cheney-style. If you are safe, and good company, you will be asked again. Anyway, I have never been much good at golf – and, as Mr M. is excellent, it is better not to compete. Plus, he insists on giving instruction all the time – do this, do that, stand with your legs further apart, and so on. (I have told him that if he gave that much instruction in bed, we would both be better off.)

So, how did I break into shooting, when I realized I needed to for my career?

I took lessons for a year and then teamed up with a friend to host some game shooting, thus reducing the cost and giving ourselves the opportunity to meet each other's contacts. Then, when I felt ready to host my own day, I asked the one major CEO I knew well if he would agree to be my guest, and booked it on a day to suit him. Then I invited other CEOs – who all came along because he was going to be there.

It worked a treat.

That was many years ago, and I am now much more established – as both a host and a guest. But that start was so valuable.

I run a successful business and can afford all this entertaining. But when I first left investment banking, I worked as an employee for several years before I was able to buy my company. During that time, I did not earn much money in comparison to my banking days, nor was I allowed much in the way of expenses.

I created a different proprietary event, which I called the MM Club, where I invited a dozen women who I admired to dinner – and invited them all to bring a friend. I paid for the room hire and the drink, but every-one paid for their own dinner. This kept the costs down and also widened my community. The MM Club is long disbanded, but my business still uses the 'bring a friend' strategy to widen our contacts.

I have also piggybacked on lots of other people's communities, looking for companies who serve a similar group of people but don't compete with my business. (Other organizations do this too – the private banking community, in particular.) We team up once a year, for example, with an upmarket fashion retailer. They open two hours early and serve coffee and breakfast in their store to the guests we invite. The result is that we are able to see masses of people between 8 a.m. and 10 a.m., and the store is able to showcase its items of clothing, handbags and jewellery to people who might not otherwise have visited. We have done versions of this – some much smaller – with several other retailers.

I have done this (piggybacking) for as long as I can remember. Twenty years ago, when I was a young stock analyst covering tobacco companies, I realized that Rothmans owned Cartier and Dunhill (now Vendôme) and they both sponsored the most prestigious polo matches played in the UK. I asked the chief financial officer of Rothmans, my own contact there, if I could take a group of their institutional investors (my clients) to the polo. They usually used these events to host suppliers and wealthy customers, but were happy to help me, and so I was able to take my clients to tea with the Queen (who in those days had tea there and presented the prizes to the winners).

In all of these examples, we tried to find venues that people would not necessarily have been to before, using contacts to secure them.

The importance of role models

Alison Platt, divisional managing director (Europe) of the healthcare company Bupa, has drawn much confidence – which is a common theme in this book – and, no doubt, wisdom from the female role models she has cultivated.

She has said about her earlier career:

> I realize now just how little I knew then. I could have frightened myself witless but what I did have was confidence, and that was thanks partly to having some fabulous female role models at both BA [British Airways] and Bupa.

The MM Club was for women only. People often ask me about women-only events.

Are they useful? Should women go?

Let's face it – if men held men-only events, we would all be up in arms.

But I like women-only events, because I think they are good dry runs for the 'real thing' (by which I mean events with both sexes), particularly because, quite often, 'mixed' equals 'mostly men'.

Internal women-only events are useful *pour encourager les autres*. They help women find role models, build their networks and build confidence – all away from the male employees of the company.

External women's events offer an opportunity for women to meet each other and build friendships as they chat to each other about things such as clothes, hair and children – none of which they would usually have in common with a man. I see them as air cover for women, while they build themselves up to mixed-sex networks, rather than as a substitute for those networks.

In addition, women-only events allow you to build relationships without people misinterpreting your intentions. At the start of your career (and sometimes even later on), efforts to build relationships with people of the opposite sex can lead to unwanted invitations. This obviously gets easier after you are married, and as you get older (and, in my case, fatter), but it is something you have to consider. I am all for using, where appropriate, what the academic and author Catherine Hakim calls 'erotic capital' – 'a nebulous but crucial combination of physical and social attractiveness' – but you do have to be prepared for the occasional downside.

Best of all are associations where the female-only network exists for something other than just to meet people.

Take 100 Women in Hedge Funds as an example. The US version of this association is a common-interest group that publishes serious work (on such esoteric things as the variation of alpha) and also does a lot of charitable work. I am all in favour of this. It fulfils all my criteria for an organization I would wish to be part of – industry-focused, and with a purpose.

Arianna Huffington is a recent example of a woman who built a successful business out of her network. Arianna founded the American news website and blog *The Huffington Post*, in 2005. She famously leveraged her network to attract thousands of A-list celebrities, politicians and experts to blog for the site without pay.

In 2011, AOL acquired *The Huffington Post* for $315 million.

Networking as an investment in your career

Building a network is about thinking laterally, trying to find a way of giving people something that they might not be able to get otherwise – access to a hard-to-get-into restaurant or event, an opportunity to meet someone they wouldn't usually get to meet, the ability to go clothes/handbag shopping at 8 a.m. (which, if you are a working mother, is very handy) – and combining this with catching up with them face-to-face and hearing their news. In the case of Arianna Huffington, she gave an Internet voice to people who, though well known, would not otherwise have had it.

What if you work for a hedge fund – or, indeed, do anything at all – and live hundreds of miles away from where events are happening?

My advice is to join, participate virtually, then once or twice a year take the time and wear the expense of getting yourself to the action.

The two most important points to remember in all of this are:

- it is in person, and
- it is about them, not you.

I am not a fan of 'network' events that are billed as such, and especially not if you are at a senior stage of your career. In my experience, they are much more useful for people starting out in their careers, and can often end up being full of people who have something to sell – especially if the organizers of the event try and make money out of the event itself.

If you want to build your network, try to do a few things that will involve networking, rather than doing it for its own sake.

Here are a few things that I suggested recently to a woman at a senior stage of her career.

- Join a livery company (these are centuries-old trade associations in London) – any of them will do – and volunteer for a committee. If you are not in London, get active in a trade association or professional body in your local area.
- Join a private members' club and attend their events. This can be a social club (Soho House) or a sports club (a golf club, a tennis club). The more prestigious the better.
- Find a charity to support where the main board is very prestigious, and where you genuinely have an interest. Most people start by volunteering to help with a specific event, then joining the development board, then ending up as a trustee. (I will address this further in Chapter 8.)

In this chapter I have set out to persuade you that you need a network in order to build your career – that what is on your CV in terms of qualifications and experience is not enough to get you to the top. I have suggested ways in which you can do this, encouraged you to over-come any hesitation you might have, and shared the things I have done myself.

But I still need to share a final piece of essential advice. In this age of email, handwritten thank-you let-ters are a way of making you stand out from the crowd. I have personalized postcards printed and carry them with me at all times to write notes to people in my net-work after I have seen them.

Be thoughtful! Be personal!

Remember that the art of building a network is all about getting to know other people – and helping them.

HOMEWORK FOR AMBITIOUS WOMEN

Whatever stage you are at in your career

Will your current network support your career?

To find out, start by writing down the names of the people with whom you exchange views and opinions (outside purely work-related contexts):

- each day
- each week
- each month, and finally
- less frequently (but at least annually).

Now, write their names on a blank sheet of paper, then join up the ones who also know each other.

Does everyone in your network – or the majority of them – know everyone else?

If they do, your network is too 'closed' to be of much use to you.

At the start of your career

Expand your network by creating your own event. Aim to do it twice a year. If you don't feel confident enough to try this homework on your own, team up with a friend and try it together. Here's how.

- Think of a venue that would give you a great rate on dinner for twenty people, and book it.
- List ten women of roughly your own age that you know, like, admire and/or trust.

▦ Email them and ask them to come, tell them what the cost will be, and ask them to nominate a female friend to accompany them. List your criteria for their selection – for example, the friend they have with the most promise.

▦ Go round the table on the night and ask everyone to introduce themselves, and to tell the table one thing about themselves that people can't find out on the Internet.

▦ Repeat from the beginning, this time asking all the women who were there the first time. And so on.

I promise you, if you do this and keep it up, you will have a network every bit as good as mine by the time you are my age – and quite possibly better.

Later in your career

Do you think you need to expand your network?
Here are a few suggestions.

▦ Write down the five best-connected people that you know well. Then ask each one to help you extend your network, even if only by one person. It will help them if you explain what kind of people you would like to meet.

▦ Seek to become involved with a not-for-profit organization where you can serve on their board, or on a board committee. Pick one where the overall board has many notable people (see Chapter 8).

▦ Set yourself a goal of meeting someone new and staying in touch with them at least once a month.

CHAPTER 3

IT IS NEVER TOO LATE

In this chapter I hope to inspire you to push yourself right out of your comfort zone.

Too many women give up on their ambitions too easily, and often for the simplest and most unnecessary of reasons. The one that is the most unnecessary of all is 'it is too late'.

I was twenty-six years old when I realized I had made a terrible mistake. I was engaged to be married for what was, truth be told, the fourth time, when it dawned on me that I should have taken a very different route in life. No, I did not break off the engagement (having been a serial fiancée for some time, I really had to go ahead and get married or no one would have taken me seriously ever again). But I did take steps to address my mistake – which was in my professional rather than my personal life.

My mistake was not to have trained as a chartered accountant. I had come to realize, four years after obtaining my undergraduate degree, that accountancy was something I would have loved, and been good at, and which would have given me credibility in my career. To this day, it is my one regret in life (in general I don't 'do' regret, just as I don't 'do' guilt – they are both emotions which use up far too much energy and can distract ambitious women).

Why did I not resign there and then from my job and apply for a training contract?

I thought it was too late. I was used to people entering the accountancy profession straight from university. I had already been in the workplace for a few years. I told myself off for not having done it when I graduated, and never even looked into the possibility of starting over at the age of twenty-six.

Much too late, I thought.

Too late?

I was twenty-six. Looking back at that decision now, I cannot believe it. I was barely out of the crib.

Not many years later, the younger sister of my Longest-Standing Girlfriend also realized, at the same age, that she should have trained as an accountant, and mentioned to LSG that she thought it was too late. LSG told her not to be so silly – it was never too late, and especially not at the age of twenty-six.

She gave up her job and joined an accountancy firm. Twenty-odd years on, she is sailing round the world with her husband, while I am working fourteen-hour days.

There is probably a lesson here.

The truth is, it is never 'too late' for anything – to go into politics, to write your first novel, to tweet, to climb Everest, or to learn to swim.

You didn't do science A levels and missed out on being a vet?

I know of a girl who took two science A levels at night school (they are much easier when you are older – it is finding the time that is tough) and then went to start her veterinary science degree in her early thirties.

What did I do, at that grand old age of twenty-six?

I applied to do an MBA instead – by some people's standards a 'poor man's accountancy qualification'. It was a great decision, and I am glad I took it. (I married that fiancé, too, and am also glad I did that.) But I still wish I had realized that it is never too late.

When Anna Mary Robertson Moses died in 1961, President John F. Kennedy released a statement praising her paintings for inspiring a nation, noting, 'All Americans mourn her loss.' Governor of New York Nelson Rockefeller had declared on her most recent birthday that there was 'no more renowned artist in our entire country today'. President Harry S. Truman once played the piano just for her.

Who was this woman who captivated US presidents and art audiences at home and abroad?

Anna Mary Robertson Moses was better known to the world as Grandma Moses, a woman who didn't begin to paint until the age of seventy-six, when her hands became too crippled by arthritis to hold an embroidery needle. She found herself unable to sit around and do nothing, even after a long life spent working on farms, so she picked up a paintbrush.

By the time of her death, she had paintings in museums as far away as Vienna and Paris.

Why do I need to tell you that story and many more? Surely, both men and women can pick up a paintbrush late in life?

The truth is, women are far more susceptible to putting up hurdles to their progress than men. Claiming that it is too late for something is the most frequently encountered hurdle of all.

Don't do it! Never use that excuse!

If you find yourself saying 'it is too late', you are almost certainly wrong.

For a start, I hate assumptions. I once read that the word 'assume' was a terrible word because 'it makes an ass out of you and me', and while that is a bit crass, even for me, it is a good thing to remember.

Never assume anything.

Women are busy people – especially if they are running the usual multitasking path of career-children-husband – and, probably because of that, are far too easily persuaded (or, worse still, assume) that their way forward is through a door which is already closed and locked.

It is never too late (or too early) to draw inspiration from others

The TV and papers seem to be full of people who have made their first million almost before they could vote. In a celebrity culture that lionizes dotcom successes run by graduates – Facebook founder Mark Zuckerberg has yet to reach thirty – you may feel that you're past it by twenty-five if you haven't already banked hundreds of thousands, if your website isn't getting a million hits a week, or if you're not repeatedly splashed across the tabloids.

Even if you are at the start of your career, it is easy to think that you have missed the boat. It sometimes seems that if you were 'just' studying hard at college, instead of dropping out and starting a business, you have left it too late.

You would do better to draw inspiration from young high-achievers who you can relate to – if you look back over *Management Today*'s '35 Women Under 35' lists, you feel like anything is possible – and, what's more, it could be you. The 2011 list had a wide range of expertise, including women in engineering, property maintenance, body-shaping underwear (amazingly, a gap in the market was found), safe sunglasses for children, designer dress rental (this would have undoubtedly helped me gatecrash exclusive dinner parties in style), wholesome snacks, and worthy initiatives such as educating children about a range of medical conditions.

The only drawback with being so young – especially as a woman – is that older men, in particular, may not take you seriously at first.

Be prepared for it, and don't let it worry you.

Louise Hodge bought her company, Pilot Flight Training, in 2004 at the age of twenty-nine. By that time, she had been flying for about five years with the school, based in Oxfordshire.

❛ I knew at university that I wanted to run my own business. I love flying, so I approached the owner of Pilot Flight Training and said, "You're getting old, you need to retire, you should sell the business to me." He put me through the wringer for about a year, to make sure I was serious, and sold it to me because he knew I loved it and would look after it. I don't do doubts – I do the thinking after I've made my decisions. I had absolutely no idea what I was doing. I learned day by day. On Day 1 I felt out of my depth. On Day 2 I said to the staff that they'd have to teach me what to do – "I'll learn from you," I said. It was rather strange, going from being a student there to being the top boss. I thought, "Let's do this together." To finance the purchase, I used money saved from my previous job in IT, plus a redundancy package. And I sold my house. It was difficult in the beginning, being both quite young and a woman. Customers often thought I was the receptionist, or would automatically turn to a male instructor. I didn't mind particularly – I had come from the male-dominated field of IT, and I thought that people would learn in time who I was. 〉

Another male-dominated industry is construction. Becci Taylor, aged thirty-one, from Lincolnshire, was one of *Management Today*'s '35 Women Under 35' in 2011. She is an engineering graduate from Cambridge University and an expert adviser on low-energy building alternatives at consultancy firm Arup. Becci actually thinks being a young woman has its advantages.

〈 If you're successful at a young age, you may find yourself telling older people what to do, be they colleagues or contractors. I have had some difficulties giving instructions to older males in the industry – for example, project managers – but I think being a young woman can often be an advantage. Young women in the construction industry may find it easier than younger men to deal with older males. Once you overcome the initial barriers, you can command respect more easily, perhaps as a result of the gender novelty. It is a stereotype, but women are often equipped with good people skills, which helps. The first job I ever project managed, I was twenty-six years old. I was dealing with contractors who were going to complete and build a design that I had started. They were experienced men in their fifties and sixties but they were not disrespectful, and they listened to what I said. I approached the situation with respect for them and their input, and without arrogance. Between us, the job got done with no problems. ❜

While being successful when you're a little on the young side can initially be a disadvantage, carefully managed it may actually be a positive advantage. Either way, it is something that you grow out of.

So, even if you don't secure one of the many young-achiever awards out there, the wonderful thing is – it's never too late!

Don't use age as an excuse

In the spring of 2009, people all over the world became transfixed by a video clip of a woman singing. In just three weeks, the video of the woman's performance was downloaded millions of times. The real surprise was that this was not a well-known pop star, but a 47-year-old unknown amateur from Scotland belting out a 29-year-old song from a Broadway musical.

No one expected much of Susan Boyle when she stepped on to the stage of the reality television programme *Britain's Got Talent*, and that's partly why her perform-ance of 'I Dreamed a Dream' from *Les Misérables* was so compelling. Subconsciously or not, we expect success from young and beautiful people. We delight in child prodigies and can rattle off youthful accomplishments, such as Mozart composing at five and Bobby Fischer winning chess championships at the age of thirteen. When someone has success, we're apt to say that this is something he or she was trained to do from an early age – after all, Tiger Woods picked up his first golf club when he was two.

That is why stories like Susan Boyle's tend to catch women by surprise. All too often, we pass certain birthdays and become resigned to the fact that the window for pop superstardom or for writing the Great British Novel has closed. Susan Boyle, an unknown spinster, has since made two albums, the first of which sold over 15 million copies worldwide.

Writing is a career in which lots of successful women started late in life. Despite having churned out loads of column inches in my twenties (for me, writing was never my main profession, more the second job I did to help pay the bills), I had not written for public consumption since I turned thirty and became a stockbroker. But in 1999, at the age of thirty-seven, I started writing the Mrs Moneypenny columns. It has hardly brought me celebrity status, but it has been a passport to so much in my life.

Many other women I know, or know of, started their writing career late in life.

The call from the *Financial Times* came as a bolt from the blue – and it didn't start well. They were planning to launch a weekend magazine, and wanted a column on 'sex in the workplace'. I explained that despite working for a bank that employed, at the time, over 70,000 people, to the best of my knowledge I had never had sex with any of them (although, with so many offices all over the world, you never knew who they might hire, so an ex-boyfriend might be lurking some-where). Equally, I had never had sex in the office – and I told them I had never misbehaved on the photocopier at office parties (I wasn't even sure where it was). It turned out that what they were really after was a column about gender, not sex, in the workplace.

I then explained that I was probably still the wrong person.

Because I do not believe in the glass ceiling – I think the best way we can smash any glass ceiling is to smash the myth that women 'can have it all'.

I put up a number of arguments for not writing the column (too busy, working mother, trying to finish my PhD), but none of them worked. I have been writing it ever since. One thing I did not say was, 'It is too late at my time of life to start writing a national newspaper column.'

Lots of women write really well, and don't discover this until later. Already a single mother, what if Joanne Rowling had thought it was too late to start writing a children's novel about a boy magician?

She might be wealthy today, but before she published her novels she was nearly penniless, severely depressed, divorced, and trying to raise a child on her own while attending college. Rowling went from depending on welfare to being one of the richest women in the world in only five years through her hard work and determin-ation, and at a later stage in life than most people start their career.

Someone who started even later was Mary Wesley, whose first published novel for adults was *Jumping the Queue*, published in 1983 when she was seventy. She became one of Britain's most successful novelists, selling three million copies of her books, including ten bestsellers, in the last twenty years of her life.

It's never too late to be 'irresponsible'

Perhaps some women (mothers, in particular) may feel it is irresponsible or selfish to switch careers or go back to school to get an MBA when it will cost the family purse such a great deal and may make family members nervous about their financial future. But, as long as you talk your family through your decision, it is anything but irresponsible to invest in your career.

At least you're not one of a growing number of 50+ women who are throwing themselves out of planes, simply because they want to. According to a charity for older people, Age UK, extreme sports among the over fifties are on the rise in Britain. While there is always a minimum age limit for people participating in extreme sports, there is no maximum! Your spouse and children would surely be much more nervous about that than they could possibly be about you going back to school or switching careers. I will be fifty the year this book is published, and am determined to invest more time in myself and my physical health. While I may not throw myself off Victoria Falls on the end of a bit of elastic, I plan to set myself some slightly less terrifying physical challenges.

Annie Clarke from Suffolk turned sixty last year and decided that the best way to celebrate this special occasion was to launch herself out of an aeroplane at 13,000 feet. As something she had always wanted to try, but had never got round to doing, daredevil Annie proved that you're never too old to try new tricks. In fact, some might consider Annie a mere youngster in this sport, with reports of some skydivers aged in their nineties – now that's what I call 'extreme' growing up.

I learned to fly an aeroplane at the age of forty-six and got my Private Pilot's Licence (PPL) at forty-seven. I didn't let age stand in the way of qualifying, even though there were a large number of written exams that severely tested the grey matter. (This included one in which I had to constantly calculate the centre of gravity of an aeroplane as I added certain items to it – as I tried to explain to the examiner, once someone my size is in a plane it doesn't matter what else you add, the centre of gravity will stay firmly near me.)

I was inspired to fly by Polly Vacher. My mantra of 'it is never too late' is wonderfully demonstrated by Polly, who lives in my village. A talented musician, mother of three and former schoolteacher, she did a charity tandem skydive when she was forty-five. She loved it – and 245 jumps later, she took up flying and obtained her PPL in 1994 at the age of fifty. Polly tirelessly raises money for the charity Flying Scholarships for the Disabled (FSD) and was awarded an MBE for services to charity in 2002.

Polly came to the notice of the world – literally – in 2001, when she flew around it in 124 days in aid of FSD. Her solo eastbound circumnavigation of the world was accomplished in the smallest aircraft flown solo by a woman around the world via Australia – her single-engine Piper PA-28 Cherokee Dakota G-FRGN. The journey included a sixteen-hour stint from Hawaii to California. I struggle to fly myself to Southend!

In May 2003, Polly set out from Birmingham to fly over the North Pole, Antarctica and all seven continents, returning just over a year later in April 2004, becoming the first solo woman flyer over the polar regions. She says:

> It's become a confidence-builder for myself, as well as for the disabled who I raise money for. I didn't think I needed it, but my confidence trebled after my first solo flight. Everything depends on how well you prepare – survival training in all conditions gave me confidence. I learned to navigate by the sun (in case my GPS failed), how to handle a life raft (since two-thirds of the world's surface is water). Of course I get scared of the unknown – the "what if?" – I'm only human.

Polly constantly encourages others to 'keep learning'. I am lucky to live near someone who inspires me so much and who is a constant reminder that, however old you are, there is always something that you can achieve in life.

Wherever you live, there will always be women somewhere who can inspire you, even if they are not world-famous.

Do you know of someone who does a lot of charity work?

Seek them out and volunteer to assist at their next event.

Do you know of someone who holds local or national political office?

Seek them out and volunteer for their office, or help out with a campaign.

You are never too old to learn – and never too old to volunteer.

It may not be an easy ride. And don't be fooled – the incredible accomplishments detailed in this chapter, and elsewhere in the book, did not come easily. Nor did they come without their challenges. I'm reminded of the German poet and playwright Bertolt Brecht: 'Those who do struggle often fail, but those who do not struggle have already failed.'

Too true.

Failure can feel like you've made the wrong decision, that it's time to call it a day. But it's normal to feel a mixture of desperation and mortification when something doesn't work out – just don't feel disabled by it. The book *Backwards in High Heels* sums this up thus:

Failure is what exposes your core of steel; it throws you back on elemental principles and gives you the chance to discover inner resources you never knew you had. It allows you to star in your very own comeback movie [. . .] In actual life, here is what failure is like: bloody awful. You will almost certainly feel it physically, as if someone has laid about you with a blunt instrument [. . .] it can come as a terrible jarring shock [. . .] You will be covered in a haze of shame.

But it doesn't mean giving up.

Carol Bartz, former CEO of Yahoo! Inc., was asked if she ever suffered from low self-esteem. She replied:

Sure. I still do. I think a bit of low self-confidence is healthy because it keeps you on your toes; it keeps you trying to do better; it keeps you trying to improve yourself in a lot of ways. I think failure's a very important part of life. Oh! You must fail! You must fail. If you don't fail, you don't know the degrees of success. I've made a lot of mistakes. There isn't one that stands out. I make mistakes every week, every month, every year, I would say. I think you need the courage to bring your idea to the surface. I think you need the courage to see many of your ideas fail. ❜

Earlier in the same interview, she had said:

❛ It's like, say, skiing. You have to fall down to learn how to be a better skier. I happen to be a big gardener, and if you don't kill a lot of plants along the way, you don't know how to garden. ❜

Enjoy being oestrogen-free

I know women are far more obsessed about their age than men. That is because your looks (your 'erotic capital') are one of your assets, and you feel their passing much more keenly.

I also know I am very sensitive to this (not that I was ever much of a looker, anyway). Last year I arrived to do a day's shooting for my TV show without make-up and with my hair in rollers. A member of the public who we were filming with that day exclaimed at how young I looked.

'They make you look so old on the telly,' she said. 'They make you look as though you were about fifty!'

I calmly explained that I was 'about fifty', and age was not mentioned again.

This brings me to another significant reason why women should never think it is too late for anything –

because we get some extra help from Mother Nature later on in life, which opens a lot of new doors.

Yes, we eventually become oestrogen-free.

Does that sound better than post-menopausal?

I have been oestrogen-free for three years, which, at almost fifty, is reasonably young to be so. But I am loving it, and do not feel in any way deprived.

Perhaps it is the knowledge that I am no longer able to bear children, and so I can direct my energies elsewhere, that makes me feel more liberated. Maybe it is just the absence of annoying hormones. Whatever it is, I feel like I have the energy and ambition to tackle as much in the second half of my working life (I expect to work to seventy-five and beyond) as I did in the first.

I have also managed to get through this change in my chemical make-up without resorting to HRT. (This stands, just in case a random man is reading this book, for Hormone Replacement Therapy – when I did my stand-up show in Edinburgh in 2010, a male member of the audience thought it stood for High Resolution Television.)

This is not because I am against HRT – I'm all for swallowing any drug that works – but because I was terrified that I would put on even more weight. The only time I wavered was when the *FT* sent me to Ireland to write a piece for the 'Pursuits' section of the *Weekend Financial Times*, and I stayed in an absolutely freezing B&B. I woke at 3 a.m. having the worst hot flush I had ever experienced. I resolved to call the doctor at first light and make an appointment.

It was then that I realized I had left the electric blanket on.

I am thrilled that people are getting out there and talking about what life is like for women after the age of fifty. In 2006, Nora Ephron published *I Feel Bad About My Neck*, a collection of essays about ageing, and in 2011 Jane Shilling published her thoughts on her own middle age in *The Stranger in the Mirror*.

In the same year, Jill Shaw Ruddock, a veritable pin-up girl for the oestrogen-free sorority, brought out *The Second Half of Your Life*, which contends that women who are oestrogen-free get their fertility in another form: the creation of ideas and purpose in their lives.

Did my life lack ideas and purpose before?

I hope not. But I suspect far too many older women don't make the most of their abilities and their time.

Reading about all the things you can try out post-menopause occasionally left me feeling quite exhausted – if I were to go in for as much exercise and as much sex as Jill advocates (the kind of self-help books I read don't tend to suggest buying a vibrator) there wouldn't be a moment left for the challenges she encourages. Shaw Ruddock clearly has a lot of energy – she has since launched a charity that will build integrated social and healthcare centres offering opportunities to people in the 'second half' of their lives.

It's never too late to find your true passion

The name Julia Child is synonymous with culinary excellence, which is why it may be surprising to learn that in her mid thirties Julia Child had to ask what a shallot was.

The year was 1948, and she had just moved to France with her new husband. She didn't speak French and could barely cook, but Julia fell in love with French cuisine and became determined to learn how to master it herself, studying at the celebrated Cordon Bleu cooking school in Paris. 'To think it has taken me forty years to find my true passion,' she once wrote to her sister-in-law.

Although she may have identified that passion, it took several more years for her hard work to pay off. It took more than a decade and 'several rounds of rejections' before the tome that Julia co-authored, *Mastering the Art of French Cooking*, was published, and she didn't begin her long-running PBS programme *The French Chef* until she was fifty-one.

Developing a new skill or interest at any age can really help self-confidence (I have already touched on how lack of confidence can hold back a woman's career). A book that sets out to look at how women can forge ahead in traditionally male work environments describes the 'imposter syndrome', where women suffer bouts of self-doubt in their careers and credit success to luck, timing, good contacts, and so on. This feeling may be compounded where a woman works primarily with men – her mere presence is 'an oddity' and her success may be considered likewise, perhaps even 'suspect'. 'If you think that success can come to you only once you are perfectly sure of yourself,' the author warns, 'you will be waiting for ever.'

I agree – and success, even if it is in an area unrelated to work, will help confidence a lot.

Francesca Halsall is a British swimmer and, at twenty-one, is already a European Champion, Commonwealth gold and World silver medallist. In an interview with *The Guardian* in July 2011, Fran appeared thoroughly undaunted, ahead of the 2012 Olympics, by the recent loss of her number one spot. She said:

> Well, I was number one in the world until last week, and then I lost it by a hundredth of a second [. . .] I actually like the fact that someone else has just swum quicker than me. It makes me step up my game.

This is a winning attitude. As much as physical condition, Fran says that state of mind is vital.

> You also need to win the battle of the mind even before you stand on the blocks. If you have the slightest doubt, you're not going to do it. Everyone has that battle but I clear my mind and, just before the start, I say something simple like: "C'mon, Fran, you can do it." And then I remind myself what stroke I'm meant to be swimming.

Having left school at fifteen to pursue her swimming career, she has now returned to studying for an A level in philosophy, at the age of twenty-one. In Fran's case, you're never too young and you're never too old. On going for a gong at the Olympics in 2012, she said, 'I'm ready to have a real crack at it.'

So, it is never too late to try something new, and that may bring confidence and career success in its wake.

What to try? I am already a great believer in personal goals, which if 'SMART' – specific, measurable, achievable, realistic and time (meaning there is a time frame) – can be invaluable building blocks to counter self-doubt.

In 2010, my self-imposed goal was to write and stage a Mrs Moneypenny show at the Edinburgh Fringe Festival (tick); the bonus was to see it transfer to New York for a week.

In 2011, I presented a TV series, which has been recommissioned for 2012.

My challenge for 2012 is to set out on the road to obtaining a CIMA qualification.

Is fifty too old to become a qualified management accountant?

I don't think so.

Does that sound like a dull way to celebrate my fiftieth birthday?

Well, it ticks all the boxes for me. It has always been my one regret, that I don't have that qualification. Others may wish they owned a Hermès handbag, or Jimmy Choo shoes, or satin sheets. Getting something you always wished you had seems to me a perfectly good way to mark a significant birthday. Plus, just the fact that I am doing it will make me more interesting – and I will get to stretch my mind. Finally, it might actually be of use to me in running my business, which is always a bonus.

So, what's dull about all that?

Retirement opens new doors

Careers can be started from scratch, even at an age when you are drawing your pension.

There are three examples of women in their sixties starting new careers in Scotland – one a trainee lawyer,

one a priest, and the other in property management –
reported in *The Herald* in January 2011. The article
started by reporting a comment on the website Legal
Week, where one would-be lawyer had written: 'I am
twenty-seven and looking to become a solicitor and
wondering if I am too old to even consider trying to get
a training contract.'

It won't surprise you to learn that this was a woman.

Too old? At twenty-seven?

Read the start of this chapter!

They also quoted an equally anxious person in
Yahoo Answers, saying 'Am I too old at thirty-one to
retrain as a chef?'

Remember, there is another even more compelling
reason why women need to banish age as an excuse for
lack of career satisfaction or progression – women live
longer than men.

I don't know why; after all, we work much harder.
But despite this, the poor dears seem to wear out earlier
than we do. Globally, women consistently live longer
than men. The gap is closing, but in the UK women still
live just over three years longer than men (to 81.9 years
of age) and in the US more than five years longer (to 80.9
years).

Retirement is a lot further away for the majority of
us than it was for the previous generation. The state of
government finances, the dismal performance of the
stock market, the ageing population – all these mean
that retirement is probably not possible until the other
side of seventy. That is what I am expecting for myself.
At fifty, I suspect I will be working for as long in the
future as I have in the past.

That is quite a prospect.

Pamela Smith, a grandmother and the first of the three sexagenarians interviewed by *The Herald*, had qualified as a nurse, a fitness instructor, studied a zoology degree and run her own business – and all this before her son grew up and started studying law. She found that she was fascinated by his textbooks and so went back to university herself, encouraged by her husband, a doctor. She was in her late fifties.

Pamela was rather apprehensive at the start of her course, not least because the average age of her fellow students was twenty. Not only did she finish her degree, she won a training contract with a firm in Aberdeen. In her sixties. I liked the quote that she gave: 'I like being part of society, I don't mind change. I'll try anything new.'

The second woman profiled in this inspirational article was Shelia Cameron, who had taken charge of her first church as a priest when she was already drawing her pension. She had spent forty years as a librarian, a career that she had apparently never really enjoyed. She had wanted to be a social worker but said 'it would be difficult to get the qualifications'. Later in life she trained as a lay preacher and then worked as a volunteer with a church in Cambridge, while lobbying bishops across Scotland to see if they could find her a job. The fourth bishop she approached was the Bishop of Edinburgh, who installed her in St Anne's. She was sixty-two.

Shonie White, the third lady in the article, is sixty and has recently, with her husband, set up a letting and property management company in Dundee for private landlords. They had retired, moved to Scotland and bought two flats as a retirement investment. Before they knew it, they were managing dozens of properties. The article said that she was planning to work until seventy, but quoted her as saying: 'But who knows?'

Shonie is fond of a saying coined by a friend: 'You don't grow old, you just change direction.'

Any age is the right age to take action

If you are reading this book at an early stage of your career, all this talk of ambitious grannies may make you wonder if it is really relevant for you. On that basis, you might as well swim through life doing very little, because you can do it all later. But it applies to you as much as anyone. As I said at the start of this chapter, I was twenty-six when I decided, wrongly, that it was too late to change direction. Julia in Chapter 1 (Yes! We are still mentioning her! That lip gloss took ages to put on . . .) retrained at the age of thirty.

There is never a 'right' or perfect time to change careers, to launch a business, or to take a risk, as demonstrated by Catriona Welsby, a young mother who set up UK-based Brand Financial Training – an online business providing learning resources for workers in the financial services sector in the UK.

My first online business (which I still run) generates a [US$] six-figure income each year. Within months of leaving my husband and becoming a single mum to my young son, I had created a hugely successful online business [. . .] I achieved this success when my life was in a mess – I left the marital home with my young son and suddenly found that I had to support us both. Unless I wanted to return to being an employee (no thanks!), I had no choice but to make a success of my business. Instead of using the mess of my life as a reason to run away and rely on an employer, I used this as a firm "reason why" to get out there. I took action and just did what I had to do to create a successful business.

How do you know if you should even be changing direction? A good checklist might be:

- Do you get up in the morning and dread going to work?
- Do you feel that you add very little value in the work that you do?
- Do you look at your boss and think that you really don't want their job?

If the answer to any one of these is 'yes', you should probably think about doing something else.

What should you do instead?

You may know this, of course. But if you don't, start by writing down lists of careers or organizations you would like to think about, and then find someone who works in that area and ask them about it. Ask people to suggest ideas for you. Keep a list in a notebook and then cross them off when you decide that they are really not for you. Once you have decided what you want to try and do, you might have to think laterally about how to get experience in the field you want to move into (I discussed lateral career thinking in Chapter 1).

Many career changes will require retraining or

another qualification. How you go about this, if needed, will depend entirely on your personal circumstances. It is always best to try and study for a new qualification full-time if you can.

You already have a mortgage?

Think about renting out your property and moving to retrain somewhere nearby where you can live more cheaply. One of my colleagues at work did this, taking a year out, renting out her apartment and going to live with her parents while doing her MBA.

You have children?

If they are young, they might enjoy living and going to school somewhere different for a while.

Your husband has a job and can't move?

Well, if you have a household income of some kind, you might consider borrowing the money to invest in your career.

But there will always be people – and I was one of them – who cannot give up their income. I studied for my MBA part-time, while working and having my first child. It nearly killed me, which is why I recommend that other people try and do it full-time if they possibly can. But if you are disciplined, and know what your priorities are, it is possible.

You will probably have to start at the bottom again in your new career.

This may not be palatable, but what would you prefer? A good wage for something you hate doing, or less money and more satisfaction?

We all spend too much time at work for us not to enjoy it. If you have aptitude and work hard, the financial differential will soon disappear.

In this chapter we have seen how easy it is to think 'it is too late', even at a young age, if you are a woman. The sheer pace of our lives, and the things that take up our time (work, children, aged parents, and so on) make it easy to shelve ambition and/or fail to address a career that has plateaued. But we live longer than men, and we have many years in which to achieve the things that we want to – even if there are challenges along the way – as the women I have mentioned show.

It is never too late to move forward, whatever your ambitions.

You can do it!

At the start of your career

How can you define your ambition?

Write down what you want to be doing in ten years' time. I don't mean 'be a VP in an investment bank' so much as 'running a team/working abroad/making more than $200,000', or similar.

Then write down the reasons it might not happen.

Then work out how to deal with them.

You need to develop a flexible approach. So, in order to do so, write down what you think your alternative career might be. As a pilot, when you plan a flight to somewhere, you always have to name an alternative airport in case, for whatever reason, you can't land at your intended destination.

Think about your career like that.

What else might you like to do if you don't pursue Plan A?

Mid career

Give yourself a career check to make sure that you are not on a plateau. Women may live longer, but you don't want to waste too much time.

Be honest with yourself – is all going to plan?

Ask yourself the ten-year question (see above) and also a five-year question.

Can you see yourself in your boss's job? If not, why are you staying?

Write down the reasons, and look at them.

Are they really strong enough reasons to keep you where you are?

If so, set a date when you are going to review them again – and stick to it.

Is there something holding you back in your career?

Write down what you think it is and then how you are going to deal with it.

Is there something outside work that you wish you had achieved?

You may wish to learn a musical instrument, or join a choir, or write a novel, or swim the Channel, or set a world record. Write down three things you would like to do, and aim to achieve one a year.

Approaching retirement

Careers checks are needed at all stages, even when you are getting near to retirement. In any case, I would advocate a 'career adjustment' rather than 'retirement' – I hope to spend the last fifteen years or so of my working life teaching. Even if you have saved plenty of money, I would encourage you to take a volunteer job.

So, now is the time for a new plan!

Write down the three careers you would have considered if you had not pursued your current one.

Why not try one of them next?

What is stopping you?

How can you deal with that?

CHAPTER 4

JUST SAY NO

No!

Say it.

Say it again.

Say it out loud.

There, see? It's not that difficult, is it?

But it is. Women have difficulty saying no, and being able to do so effectively will help you up the career ladder as much as, if not more than, any other skill in your armoury.

Why is it so difficult for women to say no?

Because, as a gender, we are conditioned to please. It seems that men have been born to perform, and women to please.

Kevin Leman, the author of *Smart Women Know When to Say No*, has quite a lot to say about why so many women are what he calls 'extreme pleasers'. He thinks that women:

- learned to please when they were little girls
- have low self-esteem
- like to try to keep everyone happy
- usually feel inferior to men, or
- have a need to be 'good girls' so that people will approve of them.

Doesn't sound too good, does it?

The issue we have as a gender, apparently, is that we are 'communal'. According to another book on the subject, *Women Don't Ask*, we are less concerned with our own needs and more concerned about the welfare of others. The authors talk about the 'good girl' or 'nice girl' syndrome, and suggest that women have been socialized to be 'other-oriented', which means they have become concerned with how their actions impact on others.

Psychologists discuss 'self-schemas' (how you see yourself). Social psychologists Susan Cross and Laura Madson argue that men tend to see themselves as independent, whereas women tend to see themselves as interdependent.

Men with independent schemas focus on promoting their personal preferences and goals, and seek out relationships that are more instrumental than intimate, more numerous and less personally binding.

Women with interdependent schemas have as one of their primary goals to seek out strong relationships and protect them. (This, by the way, should mean that women are good at building networks.)

So, we find it difficult to say no.

In this chapter, I will explain why saying no is important if you want to get to the top – and how to get better at it.

Make the correct choices

Building a successful career is all about making the correct choices. You are never too young or too old to make those choices, although the things you have to choose between change as you get older. Whether you are fourteen, forty, or four years away from your eightieth birthday, you will only have twenty-four hours in the day – and you need to use them wisely.

Time management is a subject in itself, and is addressed in Chapter 6. But before we even get there, we need to learn how to say no.

When I tell people that saying no is a key life skill, most younger audiences think I am talking about sex and drugs – and that saying no applies equally to both sexes. Life can be very tempting when so much is on offer, from a Krispy Kreme doughnut to a crafty cigarette.

Surely both sexes are tempted?

After all, ever since Eve hung around with an apple, everyone has had problems saying no.

Sure, both sexes need to learn that going out partying the night before a big exam is probably not a good idea. Saying no to something you would much rather do than study is challenging. Sure, both sexes need to learn the concept of deferred gratification, which is another good life skill. But girls in their teens want to be loved, whereas boys just want to be admired. That is why girls are such good team players and why boys end up as leaders.

These sound like sweeping generalizations – but, do you know what?

Look around you and tell me that I am wrong.

I hate saying no.

I especially hate it when saying no will affect those I love. Last year, Mr M. and I received a letter from the school attended by CC#3, informing us that his parents' day was a Monday evening four weeks hence. We both had other engagements. CC#3 was in his first year of senior school and at twelve years old was finding it challenging, so it was clearly important that we should engage with his teachers and find the best way to support him. But I told Mr M. straight away that I was not going to go.

Why?

Because that evening's engagement for me was an important committee meeting.

Surely no committee meeting could be more important than an opportunity to support my own child's progress at school?

In my view, it was.

Here are the facts that I processed before reaching my decision.

- The committee I was a member of runs an annual high-profile charitable event.
- It only meets three times each year.
- Its constituents are some of the most influential men in the City of London, all of whom could (and can) act as advocates for my business.
- It was only my second year of membership, and I had yet to add any value to that year's event as I had missed the first meeting.
- I could not send anyone else in my place.

Therefore, I made the hard choice and said no to the parents' evening.

Mr M.'s other engagement that evening was to lead the cricket coaching for the local ladies' team, something he could (and did) delegate – to CC#1. I went to my committee meeting, and Mr M. went to the parents' evening. CC#1 managed to cope with twenty-one ladies of assorted ages, sizes and shapes for an hour in the nets.

It is true that I am not keen on parents' evenings, anyway. As events they always seem to me like speed dating. You get five minutes with each teacher, before being sent off to the next one. I don't think anyone can properly assess their child's progress in five minutes (any more than they can assess a potential life partner in that amount of time). But I would have gone, if I had not ascertained that my career was better served by attending the committee meeting. And – crucially – I mitigated the risk of not attending by:

- sending Mr M.
- explaining to CC#3 why I was not going
- explaining to his teachers why I was not going, and
- going in to see them before school on another day.

Yes, I felt uncomfortable about saying no, but I have learned that saying no is important – even if I do not always feel good about it at the time.

It's a case of short-term pain for long-term gain.

CC#3 might have liked me to attend his parents' evening, but he won't thank me when I can't help him through university because my business has slowed down.

Know your priorities

I have priorities. I measure every request for my time against those priorities and, if the request does not measure up, I say no – however uncomfortable that makes me feel in the short term.

My priorities are as follows:

- my work
- my children
- my husband
- my friends, and then
- myself.

What are your priorities?

Identify them and then write them down.

Remember, priorities are different from targets.

If you know your priorities, you will know if you should be saying no to invitations.

For instance, imagine that you have agreed to go on the pre-wedding weekend of a close friend, or maybe even your sister. On the same weekend, you are then asked to be the speaker at a conference that is interesting but has little relevance for your work. Your answer, I hope, will be to say no. The conference will give you some self-promotion. But if you have been asked once, you will be asked again. You measure it up against your priorities (in my case, family and friends before me) and the weekend wins out.

But what if your sister's party is planned for the last weekend in January, and you are then named a Young Global Leader of the World Economic Forum and invited to their Annual Meeting? In this instance, there are very few women I would counsel to go and support their sister instead. Perhaps it would be better to try to bring the weekend forward, or just explain to your friend/sister that you have to pull out in the interests of your career progression.

This won't be pleasant, but it will be the right thing to do – if you want to get to the top.

Use your energy wisely

Prioritizing is key, because you quite obviously cannot be in two places at once. But even if you don't have a conflicting event, you need to remember that you should have as an overriding priority the need to conserve your energy.

Energy is the hallmark of success, and your energy comes from only one source – you.

We all need to say no from time to time, in order to conserve our energy and concentrate on helping ourselves to succeed.

I know from experience, and from the many working mothers I encounter every day, that lack of sleep can destroy energy and the ability to focus on the big picture more effectively than anything else. I recently counselled a member of my team who was doing brilliantly at work, but who failed to realize it, or take any pride in it, because she was just so tired. Her young daughter had taken to coming into her parents' room several times each night and having to be put back to bed. I tried to get my colleague to see that a good night's sleep was in everyone's interest – a successful and productive week at work would ensure a strong financial basis for her daughter's future, and that was more important than the fact that her child preferred to be put back to bed by Mummy rather than Daddy.

I suggested that she should try to get one good night's sleep each week, midweek. One idea I asked her to think about was to go and sleep in the spare room, get some earplugs and let her husband deal with the 3 a.m. wake-up calls. Another idea was to go and stay at a friend's house once a week, or bring her mother in to do one night a week.

Simple advice – but when you are sleep-fogged, you might not think of solutions such as these yourself. It is very easy to be strategic when you have had enough sleep!

I was recently asked to be the after-dinner speaker for a charity. It was a deserving cause, the invitation was well written, and the board of the charity is chaired by a captain of industry with an impressive reputation. But I said no – the event would not assist my business. Other than the chairman (who was close to retiring), no one associated with the charity or in the audience was likely to be an effective advocate. The charity itself was not in any area aligned to my business – or even to my personal interests, or my family's. The only beneficiaries of my participation in the event would be the (admittedly worthy) beneficiaries of the charity. I did not feel comfortable charging for speaking and, even if I had, I could not charge anything like my full rate, because it was a charity.

Assessing all this, I realized I was going to say no. I called my manager to run my decision past him (in case I had missed some potential risk to my reputation), and he agreed with me. He manages several – much more famous – people, and told me that they too received a lot of similar requests that they declined.

So, I did say no.

It made me feel terrible for about half an hour – it was, after all, a deserving cause – but I got an extra night at home with my family and kept my focus on my priorities. That was the best outcome for my career.

How cold-hearted, you may think.

On the contrary. I am more likely to be able to do effective charitable work if I have a successful career. The best way to help the poor, as I often remind people, is not to become one of them.

Liz Rosenberg is a woman with great strength of character – which is just as well, because a lot of her professional life requires her to say no. She knows a thing or two about ambitious women – she works for one of the most commercially successful women in the world, Madonna Louise Ciccone.

If you ever want to see the power of saying no in action, get yourself a pass to a Madonna press conference, such as the one where she launched her new teen clothes line for Macy's. The media were carefully managed by Rosenberg, who denied them the opportunity to ask questions about anything other than the clothing range. Any attempt to flout this rule – and some, although admittedly not many, tried – led to eviction on the spot. Rosenberg has perfected the art of saying no on behalf of her most famous client; something that has kept that client focused, preserved the scarcity value of her interviews, and protected her brand.

It is an example well worth following.

Sometimes it pays to say no

A crucial area of saying no is the subject of pay. It is well documented that there is a gender gap in pay. For the record, I don't think this is some male conspiracy to keep the women of the world in low-paid servitude. I think it is simply because women don't ask to be paid more.

Once again, this inclination to please, with a helping hand from self-doubt, has a lot to answer for. We feel pathetically grateful to receive whatever we are paid, and assess the other rewards for our work (flexible working, interesting occupation, sense of achievement) as a reason not to ask for more pay.

But if you operate in a man's world, you should ask for a man's pay.

If they offer you something else, just say no.

Men don't think twice about this.

I was discussing pay with a man who has a successful career working for a large international firm. He has worked there for a long time and had worked very hard in the previous year, putting many hours into key client relationships, man management and talent development for his employer. He was confident in what he had delivered and had documented it all. At bonus time, they told him what bonus they intended to give him; they even had a letter ready to hand over. He told them, very calmly, to keep the letter. He politely suggested it would be best if they all forgot that the meeting had ever taken place. He said to his bosses that he would get his secretary to put another meeting in the diary for the next week, when they could all regroup as if the first meeting had not happened. And then they could suggest a bonus figure to him.

In doing this, he signalled a very strong no to the first bonus offer. At the following week's meeting, there was a new letter waiting for him – with a higher figure.

How many women would have done that?

Most, in my experience, would have accepted the first bonus offer, and then gone and complained to everyone about it.

In a book about female negotiation, psychologist Patricia Farrell attributes women's reluctance to say no to the importance they place on relationships. According to Farrell, women have a difficult time believing that, if there is a negative outcome, it won't have a negative effect on the relationship. A woman might be prepared to walk away from a confrontation with her boss about pay, because she thinks that this might impair their relationship for ever.

There is also the problem of gender stereotypes such as the descriptive 'women are gentle' and the prescriptive 'women should be gentle'. In the business world, this means a woman has to balance behaviour that enhances a man's status (but makes a woman less popular – for example, being confident in her skills and comfortable with power) with conforming to expectation (being 'nice').

This is another way of saying that people don't like women who behave like men. We are back to asymmetric judgement: 'He shows leadership, she is aggressive.' To get the pay rise you deserve, you need to be as strong as a man would be, but in the manner of a woman.

Set a target for your next pay review.

What are you paid now, and what do you think it should be? Why?

Do some benchmarking, gather some evidence, and consider if the figure you have in mind is viable. If you work in a small business with narrow margins, it just may not be possible to pay you the salary you deserve.

In which case, are the other benefits (flexibility and so on) worth the discount?

If not, leave and get a role somewhere bigger.

If it is a viable figure, and you are offered less, just say no.

You don't have to shout, or cry. Practise what you are going to say beforehand on friends or your partner. When business leaders or politicians know they are going to be engaged in challenging interactions with others – for instance, being interviewed on live TV – they almost always practise beforehand to make sure they come across as confident, not arrogant. That is what you need to do before any compensation discussion.

Let's take a different scenario. You have been approached by a headhunter, or have applied through an advertisement, for a new role. It is a job that you would like, it represents good career progression, and it would be both interesting and rewarding. You are sent an offer for this role, but the compensation is not what you need or believe you should receive.

How do you say no?

The answer is straightforward.

You write back and explain, politely, how much you would like to accept the role, and all the reasons why you are excited by it, but you feel that the compensation is not at the appropriate level – and, more importantly, at a level that would allow you to be able to accept. You should also explain the level of compensation that you would regard as appropriate, and why.

This is not to say that you should always say no to the first offer. Executive search firms spend much of their time brokering deals between employer and potential employee. I know that they get very irritated when a candidate declines the first offer just because they assume that it is the 'opening bid'. Large employers think very carefully about the offers that they make. They start thinking about it way before the offer is made, and they discuss it with the search firm that is acting for them. They take into account the going rate for the role in the market (which the search firm will have advised them on), the compensation that the candidate is currently earning and the compensation structure within their own company.

They are rarely thinking, 'How little can we get away with?'

But some – fortunately, few – candidates seem to think this is how employers behave.

It may well be that the first offer is the right one – you should have had your target offer in mind throughout the interview process, and have discussed it with the headhunter. Then, when the offer comes, if it meets or is very close to your target, you should just say yes.

Saying no to sexual overtures

Even though it is important to be able to say no, it is not something that any woman enjoys.

Take sex, for instance.

How many of you have had sex when you didn't want to?

I am not talking about rape here. I am talking about sex in a relationship when you didn't really feel like it, but thought that saying no was too difficult. My betting is that most of the women who read this book will have to admit to knowing exactly what I mean.

Why do you think some women sometimes fake orgasms?

We are conditioned, as I said earlier, to please.

Speaking of sex, there is one important time to say no – or, at least, to very seriously consider it the default answer. It is almost inevitable that at some point in your career you will find yourself asked for a more intimate relationship by someone you work with – a colleague, say, or a client.

They may, or may not, be senior to you.

They may, or may not, be in a position to assist your career.

They will frequently already be in a relationship, often married – and you may be too.

This book is not setting out to make moral pronouncements; it is designed to help you build a successful career. Sleeping your way to the top is, let's face it, an option open to women much more than to men.

But the risks of having sex with anyone in a work environment, especially as you progress through your career and become better known and respected, are much higher for women than they are for men. This asymmetric risk is very acute – if it becomes public, he is seen as a bit of a womanizer, you are seen as someone whose judgement can be called into question.

I don't think there is any chance of this changing in my lifetime, and probably not in yours.

The asymmetric risk is not just limited to reputation; it can extend to your job. There have been many well-documented cases of senior women in corporations having affairs with the CEOs.

Let's take a moment to consider them.

How many times is it the man who resigns? (Incidentally, many of these women work in human resources.

What is the lesson we are supposed to learn from this? If you have a career in human resources, you have a better chance of an interesting sex life?)

Saying no to sex is a good career move, but this does not mean that you should hide your assets. (Chapter 9 is about the importance of doing your own PR, including looking good at work.) Being a woman can be a great advantage. Men – and let's face it, most of the people who you will encounter in your career are men – like the company of a woman, especially of an engaging and personable woman.

Harmless flirting may well help you achieve what you are trying to get done at work. I have no time for people who say that it is the thin end of the wedge, that women who flirt deserve everything they get when it leads to an unwelcome sexual overture later on. We are intelligent women, and we know where to draw the line.

Plus, what is the point of being a woman if you don't use every advantage?

I am reminded of my first year in an investment bank. My job involved calling up and going to meet dozens of fund managers. My brief was to tell them about the thoughts and opinions of my boss, an investment analyst who published stock recommendations. The idea was that by bringing his work to a wider audience than he personally had time to do, it would lead them to vote for him in an annual ranking survey of investment analysts. Coming high up in the rankings was a badge of honour for him, and for the bank that employed us. I was told that if I achieved a high ranking for him, I would get a much bigger bonus.

I consulted a younger, smarter and more experienced

colleague who was doing the same job for a different investment analyst, covering a different sector.

'What,' I asked her, 'is the key to getting these fund managers to vote for our bosses?'

'It's quite easy,' she said. 'You just need to apply the "chocolate knickers" treatment.'

'What on earth is that?' I asked.

'You need to look at every male fund manager,' she said, in all seriousness, 'as though they are wearing chocolate knickers that you would like to lick off.'

Wow.

I had to pretend that I was physically attracted to my male clients in order to achieve my short-term career goal?

'Yes,' came the answer.

Fair enough.

I am not in the business of moral judgements; I just wanted to learn how to get ahead. Provided something wasn't illegal – and didn't break up my marriage – I would give it a go.

I started taking my fund management clients out for lunch one by one on a regular basis, looking at them adoringly across the restaurant table. This worked a treat, and my boss got lots of votes from our clients in the survey.

Of course, this led not only to me putting on almost 20 lbs from lunching so frequently, but also to a couple of unwelcome offers of more than food. (It was a long time ago. I was much prettier.)

All in all, I would not recommend this as a career-enhancing strategy.

How to say no

It is essential that you equip yourself with the ability to understand when to say no, and cultivate the strength of character to do so – all in the interests of a more successful career.

So, how *do* you say no?

First of all, make sure you actually say no, and do not use some other phrase which you think clearly implies no. The word 'no' should appear somewhere, even if surrounded by less harsh words, such as, 'I am afraid that I am going to have to say no.'

Second, don't leave the door ajar in any way. If you decline an event – or an offer to check into a hotel – but say you just can't do it 'this time', you will be asked again and will have to say no again. Much better to explain why you are declining the invitation, and say, 'I am very busy at the moment with my existing work and family commitments and am only accepting invitations from charities I am formally associated with,' or, 'I am sorry, I am married and I just cannot do that,' or something similar.

That way, they will know not to ask you again.

A more intimate encounter with a colleague, boss or client will have to be declined as nicely as possible, and with an explanation. Otherwise, it will all be very awkward next time you meet. It is best to say that, of course, if circumstances were different and they/you were not married/working for the same employer, they would be the man of your dreams. It is definitely not a good idea to say what you are really thinking – especially if they are (a) senior to you and could be influential in your career, and (b) you are thinking that if they were the last man on the planet, masturbation would still seem an attractive alternative.

No to a financial offer – be it a pay review, bonus or a new job – needs to be said firmly and unemotionally, but with a detailed explanation of what would produce a yes. It is no good having histrionics when you are handed a substandard pay review or bonus, as this will only make people label you a 'typical female'. Instead of telling the person you are dealing with that you are grossly insulted, try explaining in a calm voice why you believe that you deserve a better bonus, then give them the letter back and ask if you could convene another meeting to discuss it.

If you intend to say no to a social event or a speaking engagement, and you are feeling that doing so immediately would cause unnecessary offence, you can always stall for time by saying that you have to check your diary. You don't say no straight away, which is not quite as insulting as it might be. But equally, do 'check your diary' – make your decision swiftly, to save the person's hopes being kept up for longer than necessary.

Saying no is a life skill that is very important to master if you want to be successful. But you should always remember that it won't be a pleasant experience, even when you have mastered it.

If every part of building a career was easy and stress free, there would be more women at the top. Don't expect to feel good about saying no. Even if you are the toughest woman in the world, you won't feel great every time you say it. There is, after all, a part of you that has been genetically bred to please. (It is my firm belief that, since the genders have been divided into please/perform for so many generations, genetics are bound to be involved.)

Saying no doesn't make you feel good – if you remember that, it will be easier to do it. Building a successful career (like being a good parent) is not a popularity competition.

The good news is, it doesn't feel terrible for long.

So, get over it, and move on.

Handling people who have learned to say no

Finally, a word about approaching people who have learned to say no, who are busy and successful, and whose time is very limited.

Make the request very specific, and make it as difficult as possible for them to say no.

A senior headhunter that I know, let's call her Jane Lloyd, told me how she does this. As someone who handles many sought-after roles, with over eleven years' experience in her job, she is much in demand. Yet people still email her or call her with very little more than:

Dear Jane,
My name is Maria and I would like to meet you to discuss my career.

This shows absolutely no understanding of how to get someone like her to say yes.

A much better approach would be:

Dear Ms Lloyd,

I met Mrs Moneypenny the other day at a lunch at the Savoy, and she suggested that I email you my CV.

I would be grateful if you would consider me for any roles that you may have coming up, and if you or one of your colleagues had time to call me, I would welcome the opportunity to explain more about my background and what I am seeking in my next role.

By making the ask clear (that you would accept a call from a colleague in place of a meeting with the headhunter herself) and by including the name of someone who is known to and respected by her (in this example, me), you have a much better chance of getting a positive response.

This chapter has, I hope, shown that being able to say no is a critical life skill that will free you up to meet your ambitions.

We have seen how knowing your priorities is the best way to decide if you should be saying no or not. It won't necessarily feel great when you do say no, but remember – short-term pain for long-term gain. Those fleeting moments of discomfort as you face down another inadequate pay rise, refuse to man the cake stall at the school fête, or miss a great party because you have a crucial exam the next day, will result in a much better feeling as you use your time more wisely.

And you'll have the energy to scale the career heights you were always destined for.

HOMEWORK FOR AMBITIOUS WOMEN

At any stage of your career

Do you want to train yourself in the art of saying no?

Try giving up alcohol (or bread, or chocolate) for a week (or longer), and see how you get on. It will probably he hard at first, and you may have moments when you nearly give in.

The same goes for saying no. Think of it as a 'yes fast', and just say no. Get used to saying no to things (for example, alcohol) at social events, or out with friends. It will be a good way to experience the discomfort of saying no, all the while realizing it is for the greater good.

At an early stage of your career

If you want to identify the kinds of things you might have to say no to, try this.

Write down your targets for the year – for example, get good grades in college, build a wider network.

Then list what you need to do to achieve them.

Then list what you are going to give up in order to do so.

How will you feel about saying that you can't do those things?

Thinking this through will help you to confront saying no to things more easily.

If you are a working mother

How can you manage when your children need so much parental participation at school?

Write down the ten events in the school year that most need parental participation. Do this for each child, if you have more than one at school.

Then work out between you and your partner who is going to attend each event. Agree between yourselves how you are going to manage your children's expectations.

Who else might be an acceptable substitute? Your parents? Their godparents? Their nanny? (I have used all three.)

Then make sure you market those substitutes to your children as very special people, so that when you can't be at something, and they go instead, it is not regarded as a downgrade.

And saying no won't be as dreadful as it usually is.

CHAPTER 5

YOU CAN'T HAVE IT ALL . . .

If you read only one chapter in this book, let it be this one.

I don't believe in the glass ceiling. It was removed a long time ago. The myth, however, persists and we need to demolish it.

To do this, you need to know that women cannot have it all. They really can't.

Young women today are raised to believe that the sky is the limit. I admire ambition, and I believe that women should be encouraged to be ambitious from an early age. But to grow up thinking (and being encouraged to think) that it is perfectly possible to be the CEO of a large public company/brilliant brain surgeon/concert violinist, or whatever, *and* achieve this while securing and maintaining a gorgeous husband, having an amazing sex life, conceiving and raising perfectly balanced children, keeping up your league hockey at the weekends, plus still have time to see your girlfriends and your parents, get to the hairdresser and have your nails done, and finally to your Pilates classes, is to be severely deluded.

OK, this is the deal.

Your time is a scarce resource. How you allocate it is central to how successful your career will be. If you take on board all the other things that you need to do in order to build a successful career – including the right skills and experience, the right network, the financial understanding that I endorse in Chapter 7 and the 'third dimension' that I discuss in Chapter 8 – it is pretty unlikely that you are going to have time for much else.

I am often asked if I am happy. I find this a strange question.

Happy at that precise moment?

Happy in general?

I personally believe that happiness is the wrong measure of success. I think that if we strive for happiness as a goal in its own right, we will always be unhappy. In my experience, it is simply not possible to be happy all of the time.

If what you are expecting is continual happiness, which is not achievable, then by definition you will always be unhappy. If you aim for the impossible, you will always be disappointed. In trying to have it all, you are almost certainly making sure that you will fail.

The reality of trying to be 'superwoman'

Back in 2007, Carol Bartz, former CEO of Yahoo! Inc., was the CEO of Autodesk Inc. This is what she said about trying to have it all – or, at least, trying to achieve the kind of 'work–life' balance women often think should be their goal.

❝ Where I disagree with the concept of balance is, balance in itself connotes perfection, which means that every day, I have to be a very great CEO, a great mom, a great public citizen. I should do some volunteer work, and I should call all my friends. And should call my grandmother. Maybe I should bake some cookies. So, every day I should be perfect at all of these things. That doesn't work. That puts too much strain on all of us.

I think it would be a good idea if we all stopped thinking of trying to achieve 'work–life' balance. That implies that work is not life, whereas it *is* part of most people's lives. I prefer people to think about 'life balance'. I believe that if women know what their priorities are, and spend their time in line with those priorities, they will achieve their goals – including their career goals – much more easily.

Claire Vorster is a journalist and blogger in the USA who put up this post last year.

Having it all became the mantra of the people I grew up with. We were meant to be ambitious, travel, buy at least one house, have a child or two, know what to wear and when to wear it, drive the right car, keep in shape, not grow any older than about twenty-nine, cook like a gourmet and have a great love life.

Having seen how 'having it all' has worked out for us, I have noticed this: Nobody I know 'has it all', not even remotely. Everyone has bits of their life that others may envy – a successful career, a great house, children, a good relationship, supportive friendships, health or wealth, style or charm. And they all have parts of their lives that range from tricky to impossible – a loss of some kind, a failure of sorts, a broken relationship or an out-size mountain to climb.

Claire went on to discuss Nicola Horlick, a UK fund manager who, back in the 1990s, was constantly held up by the media as the perfect career woman, even being tagged 'superwoman'. This was because she had a senior role with her employer, five children, a beautiful house in London and one in the country. Then one day she was sacked from her job and made a huge fuss about it, even travelling to Germany (she was employed by Deutsche Bank through its Morgan Grenfell subsidiary) with a posse of journalists in tow, to ask to be reinstated.

She was not reinstated. Instead, while she looked for her next position, Nicola wrote a book entitled *Can You Have It All?* which was published in 1998, and covered details of both the loss of her job and the illness of her eldest daughter who had developed leukaemia. Here is what she said at the time.

Losing my job was not the worst thing that has ever happened to me. Being told that Georgie had leukaemia was worse. Finding out that she had relapsed was worse. Having a sick child has put life into perspective for me. Before she got ill, I thought I could have it all. After all we've been through, I've learned that no one can.

I have a copy of her book. It is out of print – but before I offer to lend you mine, I will tell you that, if you read this chapter, you won't need to read the book. She went on to have a sixth child, her eldest child then died, her marriage broke up and she married again. She has never managed to shake off the 'superwoman' title, even though she doesn't think it accurately describes her.

I don't believe in the term superwoman. A super-woman is someone with five kids who has no help and no money. What I am is a capable, organized woman, who is strict about boundaries. I'm home at 6 p.m. every night without fail, and being a UK fund manager, I can be. 〕

Decide what matters most to you

Back in Chapter 1, I mentioned my friend Helen Weir, an alumna of the Unilever graduate training scheme. If you didn't know that she has a first-class degree (the highest grade possible) from the University of Oxford in mathematics, plus an MBA from Stanford, you would probably have worked it out within five minutes of meeting her. You might also guess, correctly, that she is not home by 6 p.m. each night, as she explains.

〔 When I give talks to women's organizations, I tell them that you have to accept that you make compromises. I work very long hours, but I don't work weekends, and I'm absolutely firm on that. Some people might not want to do that (work the hours), and that's fine if it suits them. Making compromises is increasingly something men are having to accept and deal with as well. 〕

Having friends like Helen can be a bit intimidating (it's like meeting Elle Macpherson, who is so beautiful that any normal woman just feels like giving up and crawling behind a stone immediately).

How could I ever emulate Helen's success?

But what I find encouraging, and even inspiring, about Helen is not just what she has achieved – I will never be able to emulate that – but how she goes about getting there. We once addressed a conference for female sixth form school students, aged sixteen to eighteen. Helen went first; the students were gripped by her presentation, and afterwards they asked a lot of questions.

I was up next and wondered how I was ever going to capture their attention as successfully as she had. But I had a trick up my sleeve. I asked them why they had not asked her the one question that I was sure they would have liked to ask.

How much does she earn?

Helen was at the time the finance director of a FTSE 100 listed company and her salary was a matter of public record, so I explained that they didn't need to ask – I would tell them, anyway. I had printed out the relevant section of her company's annual report and had it with me.

The previous year, Helen's annual compensation was declared at £1.3 million.

Given that the average age of our audience was seventeen, this worked a treat.

But what caught my attention that day was Helen's clear statement of her priorities. They were, I realized, the same as mine – but I had never articulated them, even to myself, as well as she did in her presentation. She had clearly recognized that she could not have it all, and had set out instead to attain the things that mattered most to her.

Helen's career and her family are her focus in life, and you will not find her investing a great deal of time in very much else. She does do other things – charitable activities, for a start, and taking time to watch sport (she especially loves rugby and football, and somehow managed to have her children at four-year intervals, timed to coincide with three successive football World Cups, making sure she was home and able to watch all the critical matches) – but she focuses mostly on her career and her home life.

Not all of us will be that clever – and that disciplined. I am neither. But I do understand the importance of setting your priorities and being unashamed to own them. Having heard Helen articulate hers, I went home and wrote mine down, and thereafter looked at every request for my time or my resources through that prism.

The downside of trying to 'have it all'

There are three reasons why I think that trying to 'have it all' will put the brakes on your career.

- The first is that doing anything well takes focus. When you are trying to build a successful career, focus is really, really important.
- The second is the sheer exhaustion and disappointment that will come with attempting the impossible.
- The third – which seems to be specific to women – is that if you try to balance a lot of competing demands for your time, the message you may give out (whether or not you realize it) is that you are not committed to any one of them.

Taking a conference call at sports day, walking round the perimeter of the sports ground, may indicate to the other parents (and even to your child) that you are more committed to work than to parenting. But I have had the embarrassment of doing that on a mobile phone I didn't know how to mute – and when I least expected it in the cricket match, a wicket fell and there was a huge outburst of applause.

That's the point where the client doesn't think you are committed to his/her assignment.

I have been known to book a whole series of personal training sessions, only to cancel them in order to go to sports days or client meetings. This makes the trainer think I am not committed to my fitness.

Last year, filming my TV series didn't help – not only did the rare client who is watching TV at 8.30 p.m. on a Wednesday night wonder what I was doing in Manchester/Blackpool/Bognor Regis instead of working on their assignment, I also missed several committee meetings of a worthy cause I had signed up to. In fact, I did almost all the filming in the evenings and at weekends, but it is not the reality of the situation that matters – it is how it looks.

After all that, any one of my clients/colleagues/family might be forgiven for thinking that I wasn't really focused on anything.

There often comes a time in a woman's career when she feels that she doesn't have enough time outside work to fulfil her non-work commitments. This is usually when she has a child, but it may also happen when she has a sick parent or partner. She may even have another business to run, or have become involved in too many philanthropic activities.

That's when you need to make decisions, because it is impossible to have it all.

Someone who learned this recently is Britt Lintner,

a warm and beautiful woman who raises your spirits just by smiling at you. Of Scandinavian descent, she was raised and educated in the USA and then worked in finance for many years, predominantly at Lehman Brothers in New York, Hong Kong and London. Leaving Lehmans long before it disappeared, she took a break to study fashion at the Istituto Marangoni and then launched her own fashion label. Realizing how much investment that would take, she went back to work in the hedge fund industry and invested the compensation from her day job in her business.

Like Helen, she has captivated audiences everywhere with her can-do attitude and her accomplishments. She's the kind of person you don't want to find yourself next to on a speaking platform unless you have been to the stylist, the hairdresser, the make-up artist – and, in my case, the plastic surgeon – on the way to the event.

Britt's fashion label was based on her discovery, early on in her career, that she did not have a professional, fashionable and functional wardrobe that she could wear both during and after office hours. She designed clothes for working women, with the aim of allowing them to move effortlessly from day to evening, with luxurious but hard-wearing fabrics and exquisite tailoring. Her dresses have been worn by high-achieving women from all walks of life. After President Obama was elected, Sarah Brown, the wife of our then Prime Minister, wore a Britt Lintner dress to meet the Obamas for the first time in the White House. Three of Britt's designs are worn by Christine Baranski in her television role as senior partner of a Chicago law firm in the third series of *The Good Wife*.

Britt was heralded in the media for combining a career in finance, a fashion business and motherhood. She has been described as 'both a role model to her clientele and the first customer of her own label'. I have several of her dresses and they are the nicest clothes I own. (I confess that they didn't come off the rack – Britt's staff had to visit my office with a special, large tape measure before they fitted.)

If you can't be a hedge fund manager, at least you can be dressed by one.

However, trying to do more than one thing well, especially as the pressures build, is never easy. Britt and her husband, after starting her label, had two children. Then, following hard on the heels of that big change in her life, her employer was bought by another, much bigger company, increasing the demands in her day job.

In late April of 2011 she wrote on her blog:

I don't know about you, but lately I feel pulled in every direction except the direction I want to go in, and the only way I am going to find what route to take is to carve some time out, think and write myself a letter as to how I would love my next twenty years to play out, a personal business plan if you will. I haven't done a sound check in years so decided it's time.

In the end, Britt had to choose between the day job (something she was really good at and well paid for) and her fashion label (something that she really loved, like a firstborn child). She had two real children to look after, her husband had started up his own business, and she was unable to devote the time to her fashion venture that it needed. Realizing that she had to do one or the other, and that for the time being her family was the higher priority, she decided to shut her fashion label and concentrate on her main job, her husband and her children.

This was a sad affair for Britt – not to mention a tragedy for well-heeled fashionistas of the professional world, and a catastrophe for me. I went into mourning immediately (and I have had to retitle my dresses 'vintage Britt Lintner').

Arriving at this decision would have been really tough for Britt. Saying no, as we learned in Chapter 4, never feels great, and saying no to the continuation of a business that bears your name must feel awful. Years of Britt's life, her creative work, and lots of her money, will all have gone into her fashion business. But I admire her bravery in establishing her priorities and then sticking to her guns.

I admire that so much more than keeping going, with no part of her life being really maximized.

Here is what she wrote on her blog in May 2011.

Hi everyone.

I've been sitting here hemming and hawing about how to begin this message, and because I don't know quite how, I'm just going to spit it out.

I've recently made a very difficult decision to hit pause on our dress business on July the 1st.

The net of it? As my friend Sofia once told me, 'We can have it all, but not all at one time,' and this is not my time. The inevitable fork in the road came towards the end of last year and my personal circumstances couldn't accommodate taking the leap into my dream full-time just yet.

The business outgrew the passion, the hobby and ultimately the sideline, and I simply can't do all three things any more (family, finance and fashion). What a great problem to have! Something has to give and right now, it's fashion.

Later on, she wrote:

I've learned that saying 'no' to one's ego and everyone's opinions is extremely challenging when all you want to do is say 'yes'.

How right she is.

Saying no is very difficult.

I am sure that the label will start manufacturing again one day. It had better – my dresses won't last for ever!

But Britt will always own the designs. Look at Diane von Furstenberg, who discontinued her fashion line for many years and went to live in France before relaunching it in 1997, at a different stage of her life. Her label has gone from strength to strength ever since.

The decision to focus on a few things, and especially on your career, will still not make it possible to 'have it all'. But focus is a really important part of success.

People often say that I appear to 'have it all', and I point out to them that I most obviously don't. I say 'most obviously' because I am much larger and less fit than I should be – a testament to the lack of time that I spend on myself. If I took more time to plan exercise and sleep into my schedule, and watched what I ate instead of just grabbing whatever was around in the five minutes that I get to stop for lunch or dinner, I would look totally different.

OK, I wouldn't look like a catwalk model, but I would look better than I do now.

I would also have a cleaner and tidier house (and desk) and a weeded garden.

And be able to cook pheasant terrine.

And have my aviation instrument rating.

And have paid off my mortgage.

In fact, there are many things I would like to be able to do, but life is a compromise and you can't have it all. I have chosen to focus on my business and my family at the cost of lots of other things.

Beware of giving off the wrong signals

The reason why I encourage women to give up on 'having it all' is that, in trying to do so, they may inadvertently give off all the wrong signals to their current and future employers.

Remember, there will inevitably be asymmetric interpretation of behaviour.

A study of more than 100 senior women in financial services in 2011 reported that mothers were often judged differently to fathers.

Leaving work half an hour early may be commented on negatively, while male colleagues – who regularly took time off for a sports day or parents' evening – were seen as 'champions of fatherhood'.

Think about how it is perceived if you ask for flexible working, or part-time work, after you have had a baby. I think that if a woman asks to work part-time, it could be interpreted as a lack of commitment to a job. I am not for one moment suggesting that it is evidence of that – but I believe that most male (and, indeed, many female) bosses see a request for part-time work as indicative that the woman asking for that arrangement is now part-time in her commitment to the company as well.

I do not usually encourage women to work part-time. Wherever possible, I suggest women work full-time, aim high, and reach the most senior position that they can – and then, their diary will be their own to manage.

When you want to go to your child's school play or hockey match, you just put it in the diary.

Nicola Horlick does exactly that – but even then, she doesn't have it all.

❛ I do make sure that I don't miss things like school plays, even though my children are at five different schools, and I do it by planning my diary around them. I don't have time for myself, but you make priorities. ❜

Carol Bartz works it out by allocating time between her home and her professional life.

❛ There are days when I have to be fully attentive to my business [. . .] and my family gets maybe 20 per cent of me; if I'm travelling, it gets none of me. And there are other times when it is all family. So the whole concept of balance is, as I say, catching things before they hit the floor. If I'm working on a big project at work [there comes a time when] it's time to go home and not think about work for a while. ❜

If you really need to work part-time, you might need to think creatively. As detailed in Chapter 1, I advised one woman (who had to step away from a full-time career after turning out three cost centres in four years) to teach finance part-time in order to stay current. And it worked well – she is now a senior (and full-time) financial manager at a telecommunications company.

But if you need to scale back your hours because your priorities have changed, remember that it is much easier to work part-time in an organization where you are already known and trusted to deliver. Managers are more likely to agree to part-time working when they already know and have experience of the person asking for it. Even if you are eventually going to return to work full-time, it will still be much easier to work part-time somewhere where you already know how to make things happen.

If you work part-time, one strategy that might help counter any negative perceptions is not to mention it unless you have to. Diane Benussi, founder and senior partner of a Birmingham-based law firm, explained to me how to pull it off.

Don't keep reminding colleagues that you are working part-time, as they see that as "lacking commitment". If someone tries to fix a meeting with you on a day when you are not in the office, say: "Sorry – that's not convenient for me." Don't explain. If you do, and say that you are "only" working part-time, they'll switch off. You will be discounted. A man would say that he has a portfolio career. You can't say that "I work part-time" without saying the word "only". It is almost an apology. You must be assertive – you are working flexibly.

Here we are again – asymmetric interpretation: 'She works part-time; he has a portfolio career.'

Having suggested that staying with the same employer may increase your flexibility, bear in mind that, for the really ambitious among you, staying with the same employer for too long can depress your earnings. This is one of the real reasons why women end up being paid less than men – because they don't move around as much. Women value balance in their lives – the attempt to 'have it all' – and know that it is easier to achieve that balance in a company they understand, working along-side colleagues they know, trust and work well with. In effect, they are exchanging the 'extrinsic rewards' – money, and sometimes position – for the 'intrinsic rewards' – flexibility and the familiar.

I have known women move to a four-day week and then end up being paid for four days, but doing five. In fact, I have known managers who were thrilled when a mother returning to work asked for four days. They knew that a conscientious worker would give them five days' work – and they would only have to pay for four.

Don't do it!

Think about why you want four days.

More time with your children?

Time to get your hair done?

Try to fit these other demands into your working week.

By working full-time you will be signalling how committed you are to your career.

Beware of the impact of motherhood

You can try to blame this on bigoted male employers, but motherhood can signal 'reduced work priorities' on a wider basis.

According to Cordelia Fine, in her book on gender

differences, there may be a 'motherhood penalty', even if you are committed to your career. She cites a study undertaken in the USA in 2007 in which undergraduate students were asked to sift through applicants for a particular job.

Compared with paper non-mothers, identical paper mother applicants were rated about 10 per cent less competent, 15 per cent less committed to the workplace and worthy of $11,000 less salary [. . .] only 47 per cent of mothers, compared with 84 per cent of non-mothers, were recommended for hire.

This strikes me as a bit much from a bunch of college students who would only just have left their mother's care themselves. Getting your kids to understand your commitment to your career appears vital if you don't want them creating stupid statistics in some college professor's class a few years later.

If your boss doesn't see you as committed, it can have a much worse effect than a random statistic. It can lower your confidence, and your aspirations. This, in turn, can lead to a vicious cycle. According to a book on career breaks, there is a particular risk among women who have just returned to work, when:

employers and bosses tend to be sceptical about a woman's worth. A downsizing cycle emerges: a woman's confidence and ambition stalls; she is perceived as less committed; she no longer gets the good jobs or the plum assignments; and this serves to lower her ambition yet further.

When will attitudes change towards part-time or flexibly working women – or men, for that matter?

I don't know.

But this book is about dealing with the here and now for women who want to get ahead – once they are there, perhaps they will change things for their sisters in the workplace. In the meantime, change will come when men want to do more parenting. In the UK only about 20 per cent of fathers use their paternity leave. In comparison, 42 per cent of women take their statutory maternity leave.

Laura Tenison, founder of maternity, baby and children's clothing company JoJo Maman Bébé, doesn't believe in holding your breath and waiting for what could, should or might be.

If large City institutions do move towards creating a better work–life balance for their employees, they must do that for men as well as women. You cannot be sexist either way. But I think what we may find in the future is that men will start demanding a hands-on role in parenting, and that's when things could change. [But for] now, the attitude is that it's the best person for the job and if they're prepared to work round the clock – and they happen to be a man – so be it.

The asymmetric interpretation of signals is a very real menace. While a man may be seen as stable with good family values if he puts photos up of his family in his office ('the family man'), if you're a woman, people may think you can't keep your mind on the job ('a mummy').

It is important, when you start a family, to signal your commitment to your career. When you go on maternity leave, be clear about what you want when you come back. Many employers wrongly assume that once women return from maternity leave they want a slower pace of career, so they give them a 'non-job'.

Sheryl Sandberg, chief operating officer of Facebook, thinks that the most important thing women can do leading up to a career break is to keep working as hard as they can. In a speech at a TED conference she shared her concerns that often, from the moment a woman starts to even think about having a child, she quietly leans back, doesn't take promotions and doesn't put herself forward.

Keep your foot on the gas pedal until the very day you have to leave, if that's what you decide to do. It's hard tearing yourself away from young children at home to return to work. If you don't find work rewarding and challenging, if you're bored, it won't seem worth it.

It is not possible to be the best mother ever, the best wife ever, the best executive ever, the best cook ever – at the same time, all of the time. You should decide what you want to do, and then do it. You will be much happier if you are not trying to succeed at everything.

It may be that your decision is to stop working. Or stop for a while.

This will be much easier to do if you approach it as a positive decision that you are making in favour of something, rather than seeing it as a path that you have been 'forced' to take.

Beware of harbouring unrealistic expectations

I try to speak to young women early on in their careers, even before they start their working lives, because I want them to know that they will have to make choices and that trying to 'have it all' is counterproductive at best, and the path to misery at worst.

I love ambition – and confidence, as we know, is crucial for a woman's success – but I often find that these qualities are present in young girls without the tempering effect of realism. The first two without the third can lead to great disappointment.

It is important to realize what real life looks like.

I am reminded of a young woman I know who was considering taking her academic studies forward and doing a doctorate. She spoke to a female professor who counselled her that she would have to work very hard to secure tenure (a permanent job), as secure positions were becoming scarcer. In view of that commitment, the professor suggested that my friend decide in advance if she was going to have children very early or much later, in order to accommodate her career. If later, the professor suggested that she had some eggs frozen.

At that point, when she faced reality, my friend – who was both ambitious and confident, and would have made an excellent college professor – decided that it was not for her.

There's a great lesson – if you are considering putting your foot on the accelerator, ask someone who is already a long way down the road what the realities will be like.

Are they realities that you want to deal with?

If not, you need to change direction or speed.

The Victoria and Albert Museum in London is a fabulous venue for hosting a drinks party, if somewhat beyond my budget. In the summer of 2005 I found myself there, at someone else's event, in a sea of people, most of whom I had never met. I finally saw someone I knew, in a group that included a striking-looking young woman. Speaking to her, I was captivated by her articulate conversation, her maturity, her outlook on life. A Cambridge graduate (twice over, once in Classics and once from the Judge Business School), Jennifer Harris had come to London, joined a management consultancy, realized that she didn't enjoy working for others, quit, taken up pedalling a rickshaw round London to pay the rent while she weighed up her options and thought about the longer term, and then founded her own business.

All before the age of twenty-four.

Jennifer won a Young Businesswoman of the Year award soon after that, and continues to prosper. Back then, at what by most people's standards would still be a young age, she had realized that life involves choice – and not every woman will choose a straightforward career working for somebody else.

More recently, she said:

❛ Another issue I foresee for myself and for women in general is managing to juggle a career and a family one day. I have watched ambitious girlfriends of mine quit their high-powered jobs because their roles just were not compatible with a family. I am naturally a huge advocate of women breaking through the glass ceiling but some of the careers women are encouraged to pursue, as I did, will present real challenges later on. ❜

The sooner you work out what your priorities are, the easier it will be to make a plan.

Simple, really.

Beware of the impact of your partner's career

Children may not be the only kind of career interruption that means you can't have it all at the same time.

What if your other half is equally ambitious, and gets the opportunity to go abroad?

Debra Lam is currently senior policy and sustainability consultant at consultancy firm Arup, which has offices all over the world. She is originally from Pennsylvania in the USA and is currently based in London. Debra was one of *Management Today*'s '35 Women Under 35' in 2011 – even though, in the last two and a half years, she has moved twice for her husband's career. Having started out with Arup in London, she recently spent two years with the company in Hong Kong. Debra told me:

❛ I went to Hong Kong to support my husband's career. Luckily Arup were able to accommodate me, although at the time I was thinking that this is where my career plateaus or even backslides a bit. There were some great projects going on at that time in London, and it was really challenging to start all over again in East Asia. Fortunately I met some great people, expanded my networks, and worked on some amazing projects. Then it was time to move again, back to London, as my husband had to return. And there could be another move again for me, him, or both of us. It is about compromise. But I have been very honest with Arup from the start. If anything, my husband's academic career actually helps me, as I have a great deal of experience meeting with academics, know a large number of professors, am aware of the latest academic research. This is all useful for Arup's research. My advice to those in relationships where both parties are committed to their careers is to talk to each other. Sometimes it doesn't work out, but it doesn't have to be a deal breaker. ⟩

There is a good life lesson here. Debra's move with her husband may not have been an obvious one for her career at the time, but she made sure that it helped her CV.

When I followed my husband to Hong Kong in 1994, and then to Singapore and finally Japan, I too worried that I was going sideways. But I made sure that I kept working, even if it was not in a role that I might have wished for back in the UK, and got lots of experience that came to be incredibly useful later on.

Beware of feeling guilty when you put work before family

Let's suppose you have decided not to try and have it all, and have focused instead on succeeding in the area in which your priorities lie. You have successfully negotiated with your partner or spouse so that your ambitions don't clash.

But you may still have a challenge.

If you are a mother, how do you deal with the guilt when you put work before your family in order to achieve your goals?

I have three children. They all attend different educational establishments; they all do different out-of-school activities; they are all at different stages of their lives. I simply cannot be in three places at once, and I explain this to them.

Years ago, when I was first writing the Mrs M. column, I got a letter from a reader expressing her horror that I didn't spend enough time with my children. She had also worked throughout her child's school years and he was still doing well, attending a top university. But he had suffered a breakdown before he graduated, and in therapy it was ascribed to his mother having gone out to work.

Beware, she warned me. This will happen to you.

Really?

I think not.

If anyone is going to be allowed a breakdown in my home, it is going to be me.

It was half term. And CC#1, then aged eleven, was going to the cinema with my sister. I called him and asked where he was. In a nearby shopping centre, he told me, on the way to the cinema. I immediately offered to take the afternoon off work and attend the cinema with them. He asked why. I explained about the reader whose son had had a breakdown because she had not spent enough time with him, and that I felt guilty for being at work.

'Mum,' said CC#1, 'if you come to the cinema with me this afternoon *I* will have a nervous breakdown.'

Guilt, like regret, is a waste of emotional energy.

The first thing you must do is train yourself to dispense with it.

You can stay awake until 1 a.m. worrying that your child will miss you at speech day or sports day – which means you will be exhausted the next day when you have to get up and go to work. Better to get a good night's sleep, be on good form when you go to work, and do a good job.

Your whole family will benefit from a happy,

successful mother who is recognized for her career achievements – but not from a mother who goes to work tired, is constantly on the phone to her children or interfering with the nanny's routine and, as a result, is under pressure from a dissatisfied boss.

Dispensing with guilt is easier said than done – you have to talk yourself, and your family, into it. As in the case of learning to say no, if you get used to the fact that some things will be uncomfortable, you will cope better with them.

For example, your child hates injections. But you have gone to work rather than take him/her to the doctor for a routine inoculation, which the nanny/your husband/ your partner is doing. You are sitting on the train on the way into work feeling terrible about it. Instead of sitting in anguish all the way to your destination and then calling home at thirty-minute intervals to see how your child is feeling, try reading some notes or doing some work. That way, when you get home that evening, you will be free to spend time with your child.

Recognize that uncomfortable feeling for what it is – guilt – and, having done so, remember that you are not going to give in to it. You can ask whoever accompanied your child to the doctor to send you a quick email with a summary of events, and then sit in a meeting feeling comforted that all is well.

Beware of apologizing for your choices

Finally, the best way to feel good about the conflicting demands on your time is to make your choices and own them.

I have met far too many women who apologize for being at home looking after the children, saying, 'I am only a housewife.'

There is no 'only' about this!

Being a full-time homemaker is demanding and exhausting – and can also be very rewarding, just as any career can be. And yet well-educated women sometimes feel apologetic for electing to stay at home.

In contrast, I met a wonderful, energetic lady the other day, the wife of a client, who had been to university, then qualified as an accountant, and then had a very successful career up to the point where she had stepped off the career ladder to have three children.

She loved being at home, acknowledged that she had been lucky enough to have the choice, and spoke with such enthusiasm about her life. Unlike many other stay-at-home mothers who I have met, she had thought through her answer to the perennial question, 'Don't you get bored at home?' She responded in a positive way, never once bridling at her career having been set aside.

She still read the newspapers and had conversation topics outside the realm of school choices/childhood ailments, etc. She was delightful company, but she readily embraced her life choice and was determinedly upbeat about it.

Equally, the women I know who have been happiest with a career/home compromise have been the ones who acknowledge that it is a compromise, and that they have made it deliberately. They are content to tread water in their professional life while they give their attention to their home life, or something else that needs their time and focus. They have chosen to do this deliberately and have a view about when they will return to putting their career first.

In this chapter I have set out to explain why 'having it all' is impossible, and how best to achieve a balance in your life that works for you.

If you want to achieve career targets (or, indeed, any other targets), something else will usually have to make way. Every woman needs to be able to set her priorities, and should judge her time allocation between them.

The most important thing is to know what you want, and why, and then make your choices accordingly.

You can't, I am afraid, have it all.

At any stage of your career

How to work out your priorities

Write them all down.

Now, write the list again, this time in order of importance. If you have more than five, reduce them. And remember that the first two will take most of your time.

Make a date in your diary to review them – in two years, perhaps?

Our priorities change all the time.

Just like making a will (something you should do, and review each time your life changes), you need to keep your list of priorities current.

How to work out if your priorities and your time are in sync with each other

Analyse a typical month.

How much of your month do you spend on each area of your life? (Just to give you a start, I spend a third of every month asleep, and 5 per cent of it commuting to work.)

Now, compare it to your list of priorities.

If there is a mismatch, work out what you are going to do to rebalance it.

If you feel you are constantly failing to achieve one of your goals, it may be because your goals are not supported by your priorities.

What are your career goals and targets?

List them on the left-hand side of a piece of paper, then put your priorities (see above) next to them.

Do you think one supports the other?

It is no good having your career as your top goal if your family are right at the top of your priority list.

Go back and rethink both lists until they are more evenly matched. (I would also point out that a successful career will usually benefit your family, so they may not be incompatible in the long term. But, for this exercise, look at the short term.)

At the start of your career

Check that you are willing to make the sacrifices necessary to get where you think you want to go.

What is your five-year plan?

What is your ten-year plan?

Go and ask people who are already there.

What did they have to do to get there?

Are you prepared to do the same?

If not, adjust your goals.

A working mother

Are you suffering from working mother guilt?

Here's a way to try and cope with it.

First of all, know that working mother guilt is usually 'unhealthy' or 'inappropriate' guilt (i.e., when you haven't done anything wrong).

Then, when you are feeling bad about something, stop and consider the following things.

- Is your guilt rational? You might think that mothers who are not there to read their children bedtime stories every evening will be holding back their child's normal development. There is no hard scientific evidence for this. Whatever you think you are doing wrong, check the evidence – if it doesn't back you up, you can stop feeling guilty.
- Does your guilt have a 'restorative' purpose? Are you going to change your behaviour as a result? If your child does something naughty and is told off (lies, crosses the road alone, is unkind to another child, or any other behaviour that needs to change), you will be pleased that they feel guilty, because it will reinforce better behaviour. The guilt will have been 'restorative'. But if you can't take your child to school in the morning because your work hours won't allow it, and you want to remain in your current role, it is pointless feeling guilty about it. It will not change your behaviour, because you will still have to go to work before the school run.
- Is your guilt about you, or your children? Do they mind if their birthday cake is bought or home-made? Or do you just want to tell the other parents that you baked it, or feel proud of your own achievement? If it is about you, the guilt is not worth feeling.
- Is it short-term guilt? Look at the long term. Will your children benefit from your career doing well in the long term? If yes, then it is worth feeling a little uncomfortable as you go along. Think about the

physical training that needs to go into achieving a sporting goal, such as running a marathon – you know that there will have to be some pain along the way. It is the same with careers.

If you have gone through all of the above and still feel dreadful, it's time to share your concerns with someone else.

Ask them if you should be feeling like this.

Chances are, the answer will be no.

CHAPTER 6

. . . BUT YOU HAVE TO DO IT ALL

As a woman, you will almost certainly have to cram more into your day, week – and even life – than a man.

Why?

And how can you stop it derailing your career?

This chapter specifically addresses working women with children, but it equally applies to caring for aged parents, or a holiday house, or a relationship that you would like to invest time in, family that you want to see more of – indeed, anything at all that needs attention other than your job. This will be whether you go out to work, don't work, or even if you are the only person working, with a stay-at-home husband.

Women with careers have to cope with more than men do. Just ask Justine Roberts, who met her good friend Carrie Longton when they were both attending the same antenatal classes. Later on, after a stressful and supposedly 'family-friendly' holiday with her one-year-old twins, Justine went to Carrie with the idea that they should set up a forum for mothers to share information with each other. The result was Mumsnet, a website which by the summer of 2011 had 1.5 million unique users every month and 25,000 posts a day – most of them from mothers in the UK. It is now a major voice, and its popularity with politicians is a testimony to its influence (the general election in the UK in 2010 was dubbed 'the Mumsnet election').

Justine, now in her late forties, started her career as an analyst for an investment bank and then later turned to sports journalism. She is married to a journalist and has four children. When she started Mumsnet, she ran it from her spare room for five years before it eventually moved out into its own offices. Mumsnet now employs thirty-five people, mainly part-time mothers. (Can you imagine how organized and tidy that office must be?) With that much data available to her, Roberts is frequently approached for comment on issues around motherhood. In June 2011, this is what she said in a newspaper interview.

> I am convinced – and Mumsnet surveys bear this out – that even working mothers still pick up the bulk of the domestic responsibilities [. . .] we're still making the playdates, arranging the birthday parties, dealing with the childcare. The school rings me if there is an issue with the child: they don't ring my husband.

According to the UK government's Equalities Office, women are still the primary carers when it comes to looking after children, and they make up around 90 per cent of all lone parents.

Here we are in 2012, and women still bear the burden of responsibility for the lion's share of domestic work – and this is even the case where both parents are working. The authors of *Through the Labyrinth*, a book on women's leadership, remind us that '[w]omen's tasks are more frequent, routine, and difficult to skip, and this lack of flexibility contributes to women's burden'.

Don't assume that, just because you're earning and/ or working longer hours, your partner will do more housework. On average, in the USA, men do one hour of housework to women's 1.7 hours and one hour of childcare to women's 2.1 hours.

Chances are, your husband is employed too – so he may be almost as busy as you are. While a partner may help out in your absence, if you are both present at home, in all likelihood you'll have to watch the baby and probably cook the supper too.

I didn't need to read any books to know this – I have been married for a long time.

I believe there are three reasons why women continue to bear the major share of household administration and childcare responsibilities – even when both parents work, or in cases when only the mother works.

The first reason is that we are good at multitasking – in my view, so much better than men. (This gut feeling is not borne out by any research, by the way. In fact, there is a whole body of work which says that multitasking can be damaging for performance.)

The second and third reasons are a direct result of social conditioning: 1) men expect women to do all this, and 2) even worse, women expect to do it as well.

The power of social conditioning

This book is about the here and now, not about the world as we would like it to be. Men have been raised, on the whole, to expect women to do things for them.

Do we wish they had been raised differently?

Sure.

Those of us with boys need to think about how we bring them up, to avoid this.

DeAnne Julius is an astute blonde whose career has taken her from the payroll of the CIA to setting interest rates at the Bank of England, and beyond. Despite having passed her sixtieth birthday, she sits on several international public company boards and continues with a very active working life.

I was once asked to speak to the women's network of a high street bank, which held quarterly meetings. DeAnne was a speaker at one of these meetings, so I thought I would go along and get a sense of how it all worked, hear the kinds of questions that she got asked, and so on. She showed a number of PowerPoint slides, which only re-inforced what I already knew – namely, that she had scaled career heights through being highly focused, building an enviable network, and was financially very well educated – all the things that I espouse in this book.

But her last slide made me sit up and really pay attention.

'Are you raising an equal opportunities household?' it asked. 'Or are you, as a woman, still doing everything for everyone despite the fact that you go out to work?'

I suddenly realized that I was guilty as charged.

I have never raised an equal opportunities household. Ever since my three boys were born, I have looked after them as well as I can, running round after them, picking up their toys, cleaning their rooms, putting meals on the table, and so on. All three of them went off to boarding school at a relatively young age, where every night they handed in their shirt, socks and pants and . . . Lo! A clean set appeared at the end of their bed the next morning, put there by the Laundry Fairy.

I sat glued to DeAnne's every word.

'Remember,' she said, 'you will be amazed how much a child as young as six can do in the house.'

In DeAnne's house, apparently, they have a strict rule – whoever cooks the meal does not clear the dishes or wash up. I went straight home and made the Cost Centres unload the dishwasher.

Of course, it was all a bit late – and I apologize here and now to the three women who will marry them one day. If you have sons, and you also want a different world for your daughters (and those of other people), please remember this. Even if you have only daughters, the example you set by looking after your husband too well may perpetuate from one generation to the next the idea that women have to do it all.

But this is not a parenting book – it is a book for women who want to reach the top.

Be prepared for asymmetric treatment and attitudes

I was chatting recently to a woman in her late thirties – a senior executive, married with children. Let's call her Stephanie. She told me:

> I'm not treated equally at work. After two nights in the office until three or four in the morning, I asked to leave as I felt I wasn't needed for anything else. My boss says to me, "Yes, you should get home to your children." My male colleagues have children too, but they would not get this kind of response from him.

This is as asymmetric as it gets, in my view.

I remember the same thing happening to me about

six months after I was married. Everyone was working late on an important share-offering document, and someone asked me – and only me – if I needed to get home to my husband.

Who, they asked, was cooking his dinner?

I took my wedding ring off that night and have never put it back on (except, of course, if my mother-in-law is visiting from Australia).

Miriam González Durántez, wife of the UK's Deputy Prime Minister, was asked in an interview how she coped with a job and three children – especially when her husband had such a busy job. She rightly pointed out to the interviewer that this was a question that implied that it was her responsibility, rather than his, to balance everything.

> Nobody would ask him how he balances everything. For some reason, there is a kind of assumption in your question that it is my role to balance it.

Why did no one ask him how he coped?

After all, he had three children, and a wife in a senior job.

It seems nothing is likely to change – for a generation, at least – and we had better get on with doing everything, and expecting to.

Tackling the reality of a stay-at-home husband

Stay-at-home husbands are going to be more the norm in the future, especially for women who are headed for the top.

In 2010, Mr M. decided to give up his full-time job as a wine merchant and look after the children while retraining as a cricket coach. We have not had a cleaner since the credit crunch, and we didn't replace the au pair. I was rather worried about this new state of affairs, and said so in my column.

Would it work?

A torrent of letters came back from my readers, relating how they too had dealt with similar changes in their households. One of them, from a lady I will call Liz, was both eloquent and humorous, and told her story straight from the heart.

She explained that when her husband was made redundant in 2007, two years ahead of the earliest possible date he could have retired, she went out and got a full-time job, despite not having had one for many years. She was a lot younger than her husband and knew that she probably had twenty years or more to contribute to the workplace.

Her husband agreed that he would stay home and look after the house and the children, who were all in senior school. The family were down to only one pet, so Liz thought it was as good a time as any to try a role reversal. She then allocated tasks between them.

Her husband agreed to:

- clean the fridge (and learn when it was necessary to do so)
- wash and hang out the wet washing in a way that minimized ironing
- clean the house during the week to get rid of visible dirt and clutter (except the children's bedrooms)

- walk the dog once a day
- shop for daily essentials
- cook (this apparently took a little effort)
- read and act on all communications with the school
- check school homework was done
- check the children got to medical appointments (although Liz remained responsible for booking and, if necessary, rebooking those appointments)
- occasional gardening.

Meanwhile, Liz kept the following tasks:

- window cleaning
- ironing
- washing silk and wool (she took this on after losing a cashmere twinset)
- shopping for children's clothes and shoes (her daughters were in their late teens, so she felt she needed to supervise shopping)
- all official paperwork (for example, passport renewal, tax returns, library books)
- looking after her car.

Liz then wrote out tasks for everyone – to save having to tell everyone what to do – and included it in her email to me.

It made compelling reading.

But when you read the two lists above, you realize that Liz had gone back to work and still had to retain many of the responsibilities she had had before. She was, in effect, doing it all – including managing a household staff (her family).

How did she cope?

In her own words:

❝ I have taken the advice of my sister ("If you can't get a cleaner, then live with it!") and a therapist ("Your situation is like driving on clear ice. If you complain, it is like hitting the accelerator or stomping on the brake on clear ice . . . it will not achieve the desired result"). ❞

Liz tried to explain to me how she felt about her 'doing it all' situation: 'In my head I wish for quiet and peace and free time, but in my life I just carry on.' She does feel quite overwhelmed at times – especially when she realizes that she is the only person who stands between the whole family and penury – but she says that when she gets to the office and remembers how much she enjoys working, she feels better: 'I like my job, and it is better than all the part-time things I did before.'

Liz has also had to cope with things not being done as well as she would have done them. 'You notice some badly turned-out children in the street, and suddenly recognize your own son.'

Liz is a good example of what the book *Spousonomics* suggests – namely, a comparative advantage approach to dividing up domestic chores, whereby efficiency is taken into account rather than a 50:50 division. She has also clearly learned the key to successful outsourcing – don't expect things to be done as you would do them. Instead, learn to live with things being done differently.

Each of us has our own boundaries. We need to make sure that, when we delegate things, whoever is in charge knows what those boundaries are. I, for instance, can live with the bed being unmade, or the laundry not done, or the car not booked in for its service. But Mr M. knows that if I come home at the end of the week to find the post has remained unopened, I will have a total sense of humour failure.

Ann Moore, former CEO of Time Inc., has been married for many years and has one son. She heartily endorses a blend of work and home life, but warns: 'Find your own balance, and be happy.'

On the subject of sharing domestic duties, Ann recalls how differently she and her husband shopped for 'necessities'. When Ann became a mother in 1984, she and her husband would make lists for the housekeeper of the most important staples they needed in the house: 'Never did my husband's and my list overlap, even by a single item.' Her list included necessities such as diapers, eggs, milk, toilet paper. Her husband listed macadamia nuts and Welch's grape juice in his top five. 'We have to live with it,' Ann says. 'There are differences. That's just the way it is.'

Similarly, your nanny will not do the things with your children exactly as you would. Your husband will not necessarily clean the fridge or change the bed sheets when you would have. If you are going to outsource, especially to a stay-at-home husband, you must teach yourself to care less.

Some women who wrote to me thought that the house-husband idea would just end in tears. Here are the thoughts of one woman – let's call her Catherine.

I read your column this week with some concern. You imply that Mr M., newly retired, will be able to replace the 'army of external childcare support' you have previously employed. I do not wish to throw cold water on what appears at first blush both an economically sensible and personally satisfying decision but I would issue a word of caution.

Some years ago my former husband and I optimistically went down the same path, with only two cost centres. You may find that, in addition to the small print in the school paperwork, such as the first day of term, PTA meetings, exam dates, etc., other details such as nail clipping and teeth cleaning may occur only spasmodically without your (or an au pair's) supervision.

She continued with another warning:

Additionally, topics for conversation narrow. I know that you have worked in an investment bank and fly a plane so you no doubt have endless anecdotes for the dinner table but you may find it less than stimulating to learn that Mr M.'s day was enlivened by someone accidentally checking out the items in his supermarket trolley or Blockbuster closing early.

You may therefore want to encourage golf or other sporting interests but bear in mind that this will only cut down on his ability to accomplish even the larger tasks, such as taking the younger CCs to and from school/sport, etc., and will certainly foreclose any possibility of mastering details.

There is simply no (unmedicated) way to avoid either the frustration of seeing so little accomplished in a working day or the jealousy of seeing him relaxed and unperturbed by what is left undone. I urge you either to send him back to work or to continue to employ your army.

Note Catherine's mention of a 'former' husband. She is now the payer of copious alimony.

There are plenty of women who *have* made it work, though.

Angela Braly, chairman, president and CEO of Well-Point Inc. (WLP), who is married with three children, often credits her husband for staying at home to raise the kids while she pursued success in her career. 'I so appreciate the choice that he's made – and he's so good at it.' She points out that most people seem to raise an eyebrow when the father rather than the mother stays at home, and are unsure – like my reader Catherine – if it will work. Angela says that, in her case, 'It's fabulous, it works really well.'

Angela is not the only one – there are many more.

The husband of chief executive of PepsiCo, Indra Nooyi, left his full-time job and became a consultant in order to work more flexibly and be available to support his wife.

When Angela Ahrendts, Burberry's chief executive, had to relocate from the USA to London, her husband Gregg (who she met in elementary school – I love that story) had to shut down his own successful construction business and move to the UK to manage the family. His experience has proved invaluable in renovating the large neo-Georgian pile the family has bought in countryside to the west of London.

Patricia Woertz, CEO of Archer Daniels Midland, credits her ex-husband, a logistics consultant, for making the sacrifices that allowed her to keep climbing the corporate ladder. 'At one point, we sort of said to each other, "Gee, somebody's career is going to have to take priority,"' she says. They chose hers.

That is also what Helena Morrissey, CEO of Newton Investment Management, and her husband agreed to do. Helena's husband, a journalist, is a stay-at-home husband and they also have a nanny. Helena says,

'Maybe there is a sense of slight stigma if men stay at home, but I think it's one of the things that definitely helps unlock that pipeline of women.' She has urged women to talk to their husbands about which of them should give up or scale back their career to take on more childcare.

I totally endorse this approach.

There is no reason why it should be the woman who gives up her career. You should have a full and frank talk with your husband or partner, and decide whose ambitions will support the family better in the long run.

There will inevitably be challenges in a marriage with a stay-at-home husband that will probably not arise with a stay-at-home wife. A stay-at-home husband is likely to feel totally exhausted and ready to hand over the management of the home and children the minute the weekend starts. (We are back to the asymmetric treatment of women here, of course.)

Can you imagine a stay-at-home wife telling her hard-working husband when the weekend starts that he is in charge of everything – kids, cooking, the lot – until he goes back to work on Monday?

Of course not.

In fact, he often gets to play golf on the weekends – and probably does very little childcare, as he needs a rest after all that week's hard labour in the office, foreign travel and so on. But in the reverse situation, where Mum is the breadwinner and comes home exhausted on a Friday, she will often take over to give her husband a break.

Stephanie, who I mentioned earlier, is the sole bread-winner in her family and her husband stays at home to take care of the children.

How is it working out?

Prioritizing is key. Having kids makes you much more brutal about making decisions. But I have been known to stay up until 1 a.m. making a cake or sewing jeans – because I feel I should, even though my husband is a stay-at-home father.

Note the word 'should'. There is really no need for such a word in the vocabulary of any working woman. 'Should' implies that you are trying to live your life through other people's eyes, not your own.

Stephanie explained:

I do have a sense of responsibility for things outside of work that my male colleagues don't. On a Friday I feel the need to slot back into my Mum role and shed my corporate cloak; at weekends I take over completely from my husband – that's the deal. You need to be good at shutting doors to other areas of your life. It's what I want to do – my break is to spend time with my kids. Communication between us is key – and observing boundaries; sticking to the deal.

She went on to say that a lot of people make judgements about her working while her husband stays at home. I suspect it is judgements like these that stop many couples following the same path.

Maybe Stephanie is right and her 'break' is caring for her kids. I am more inclined to think that she is just doing too much.

Resisting the pressure to be 'supermum'

Some of me suspects that the real issue is the pressure that other women, and the media, place upon women, working or otherwise, to be 'supermum'.

I will always remember the day that one of my colleagues sent an email to the whole office with a great brownie recipe that took very little time to put together: 'I made these last night between putting my cost centre to bed, cooking for my in-laws, packing for our holiday and doing some work!'

She was trying to share with us a time-saving tip – all I could think of was a) how exhausted she was going to be if she kept that up, and b) instead of emailing us, she could be going to sleep!

Historically, women are spending more time today with their children than their grandmothers did – and this is true even when women work. There is huge pressure to interact with children – perhaps a direct result of the influence of the media and all those mothers blogging on the net – but employed mothers in 2000 spent the same amount of time interacting with their children as non-working mothers did in 1975.

Moreover, parenting pressures are most intense among mothers who have the most career potential. Because educated women tend to be particularly critical of their own parenting, they spend more time with their children than do their less well-educated counterparts.

Harness the power of outsourcing

What is the secret to multitasking well?

Simple – you *must* learn to outsource.

Outsourcing is, self-evidently, key to a successful career.

Baroness Virginia Bottomley, currently chair of board practice at headhunting firm Odgers Berndtson, spoke at the launch of a gender diversity study in early 2011. She said: 'If you want a high-flying job, you've got to get some high-flying help. If you want to have it all, invest in domestic structures.'

So, none of this 1 a.m. cake baking or jeans sewing. Buy the cake and be proud of being able to afford to do so. Send the jeans to the dry cleaner's to be hemmed.

Own your choices! Get over your guilt!

When you are really successful, the housekeeper can bake the cakes.

Will your children be in therapy in twenty years' time, bemoaning the fact that Mum didn't make her own cakes?

I doubt it.

Jenny Knott, CEO of Standard Bank, was keynote speaker at the launch attended by Virginia Bottomley. The audience was mixed, but much of what she said related to her own experiences as a woman, and so her advice was directed at the ladies present: 'You must learn how to delegate and not be ashamed that you can't do it all. You just can't be superwoman.'

My views on outsourcing are not popular with some people, and I well remember a woman in the audience at an event of mine who said she was not going to pursue her career if it just meant that some other woman was going to live in servitude cleaning her house – how was that progress for women?

Firstly, we should all take pride in the work we do – whether it's cleaning or running a company – so I don't see earning a decent wage through domestic service as a form of enslavement. Besides, domestic help may even come in the form of a man – you never know!

This book is about progress for you, not for women as a whole – although if, as a result of reading my book, a few more women get to the top, it will have served the wider cause well. If you have a senior well-paid job yourself, you will probably have created several jobs, and many of them may have been for women, which will be a good thing. The cleaner you employ may well use the money to educate her children. As a woman I have doubled the size of my business and the number of women employed in it (as they are almost all women), plus outsourced a lot of domestic tasks.

All of this has created employment, direct and indirect, for other women.

Find the childcare/homecare solution that works for you

The authors of *Backwards in High Heels* warn that 'leaving your child with a virtual stranger is a very peculiar experience indeed' and that many mothers are not equipped to deal with the 'strange relationship' between a mother and a carer.

For many women, their inability to get to grips with the work/nanny conundrum can be instrumental in their decision to stop work altogether: they can feel a strong need to reassert their authority as mothers.

In October 2010, the Huran Report announced its list of the top twenty self-made women billionaires. Interestingly, eleven out of the twenty are Chinese. While a portion of this success is the result of economic growth, a greater part, as noted by the *Financial Times*, is the result of the ambition of Chinese women. According to a study by the Center for Work-Life Policy in New York, 76 per cent of women in China aspire to top jobs, while just 52 per cent do in the USA. The centre believes that women in China and other emerging markets 'are able to aim high, in part because they have more shoulders to lean on than their European and American peers when it comes to childcare'. In these countries, childcare is both cheap and stigma free, so women can outsource their home life.

Over the years, I have been fortunate enough to have had a few excellent nannies who have stayed with me for a long time. I realize that some people may hate the thought of outsourcing their childcare – be it to a nanny, day care centre, preschool, after-school care, or by any other means – but I firmly believe it is much better for children than stressed parents.

Do you feel guilty about putting your child into day care, or hiring a nanny?

Guilt has no place in the life of a career woman (see the 'homework' section at the end of Chapter 5).

Because a really effective nanny allowed me to be

very effective myself, I ran an incentive pay scheme – the nanny received a six-month bonus which went up a little each time (in effect, a backdated pay rise). I laid out in writing when the nanny arrived what really mattered to me, so that no one was in any doubt. I also made it clear that (other than establishing quite a long list of ground rules) I would not micromanage her.

In other words, I put as much effort into thinking about my nanny and her pay and development as I put into my employees in my professional life. This is echoed by Catherine May, group director of corporate affairs at Centrica, in her domestic arrangements. She told me:

‘ A lot of women complain that cleaners miss important details – hoovering under sofas – but people seem to find it hard to give clear directions to domestic help. Oddly enough, they have no compunction about it in the office in their professional role. I think domestic staff should have annual reviews and job appraisals and be treated as professionals in the same way we treat colleagues in the office. ’

I like my bed linen to be ironed (mainly because the sheets have such a high thread count), whereas the rest of the house doesn't get such pampering. Mr M. – like the nannies/cleaners before him – didn't take well to ironing sheets, so they go to the laundry. The laundry manages to break or even lose buttons on my duvet covers, but at least they collect and deliver and the linen is ironed.

The grocery shopping can be outsourced online (in the UK and parts of the USA). This is not always perfect, especially if they haven't got things in stock and make strange substitutes (no, I don't want organic multi-seed high-bran bagels instead of the plain white ones I had ordered – this is not a tantric yoga commune), but at least I have not had to spend a couple of hours grocery shopping.

Another thing that can be outsourced is the family's social planning and household tasks. For just £49 per month, lifestyle concierge services such as TEN and Quintessentially can arrange dinner reservations, handymen and holiday gift purchases.

Are the in-laws coming to town, and you just don't have time to make a dinner reservation far enough in advance?

Shoot a quick email to the concierge and they'll have it done in a jiffy.

Now, take an inventory of everything that you need to get done in your life on a regular basis – is there someone who could do it instead of you?

One of the best things I ever did was open an account at the local taxi service, in 1998. If one of my children is stranded somewhere, or I need to get to the station in a hurry, or I have lost my keys and need the duplicate set brought to me from home, they are the solution.

Be organized and use time well

I remember when I received my honorary degree from the University of East London the other honorary graduate that day was the (male) founder of a large greetings card company, a successful man in his seventies who had worked his way up from nowhere to great wealth and success.

In his address, he told the thousands of students graduating that day: 'There are twenty-four hours in the day. Use them.'

His view was that men need six hours' sleep a night, women seven and children eight.

Any more than that, and we are wasting time.

I agree that every hour in the day is there to be used. Nothing irritates me more than feeling that I have wasted my time. The direct consequence of this is that I barely even go to the loo without some paperwork to read. Loo seats can be very comfortable and cubicles very quiet – so, when nature calls, take advantage of the time to do some paperwork away from your bustling open-plan office. I highly recommend it.

I am always keen to learn about things that might save me time. People often ask me how I manage everything – the business, the writing, the teaching, the charity work, my three Cost Centres. It's not that much, really. If you add in an Australian husband who really cannot understand why people need to wear top hats to go to Royal Ascot ('I look like an undertaker – what do the British think they are playing at? I could have bought a new golf club for the price of this hat!'), I suppose it does look like a lot to handle.

My top tip for busy working women is to learn from other people how to save time.

I will be forever grateful to the person (herself a working mother) who taught me that by pressing the letter 't' at any time on your BlackBerry you go straight to the top of the email pile, or, if you are already in an email, straight to the top of the email itself.

In turn, here are two of my own top tips for saving

time if, like me, you are trying to multitask faster than a Cray computer.

■ First, take a laptop to the hairdresser, especially when you are having your colour done. The wonderful thing about hairdressers is that there are power points at every seat. Of course, this is also a credit-crunch tip – when we start to leave the recession, I will return to the ultimate time-saving measure with hair, which is to have someone come to the office. This tip also works with manicures and other beauty treatments.

■ Second, take taxis from time to time instead of a) the tube, or b) driving yourself. This allows you to make those three extra telephone calls that you wouldn't otherwise have time for. My children, my parents, the business call that is not time-sensitive but probably reputation-building – these are all beneficiaries from being above ground and not driving myself. It might cost money, but the gain will be invaluable.

As the recession ends, consider having yourself driven regularly. Not many businesses can justify a full-time driver, but chauffeurs cost less than you think. Any evening with more than two must-be-seen-at drinks parties justifies the expense: there is no need to check your coat, you can leave your bag in the car (as well as reserve supplies of business cards and spare pairs of tights), and you can look generous by offering to drive people home in something better than a minicab.

Diane Benussi, the Birmingham-based divorce lawyer, agrees with me.

❛ Get yourself a driver – you never have to worry about a car and, crucially, can glide in and out of meetings without the stress of driving, navigating and parking. If paid by the hour, it is cost effective, because you can work longer in the car and earn more than the driver costs you. ❜

Time management is a well-covered topic in academic and management literature, and there are lots of courses that you can attend. But time management for women is a very particular skill, because we are combining such a variety of tasks rather than just dealing with an overburdened in-box at the office.

Ruth Klein's book on time management for women has a long list of suggestions, including a comprehensive forward-planning diary. I run this too – a paper diary listing domestic arrangements (orthodontist appointments, weekend social engagements, school exams, when the flea treatments for the dogs are due, and so on) plus all my travel and evening appointments, which my assistant, Observant Olivia, emails home each day.

Learn to 'integrate or suffocate'

One of Ruth Klein's suggestions that I particularly like is one I have been practising for years without formally describing it.

This is what Klein calls 'integrate or suffocate'. She lists several specific tips on how to integrate family and work or home commitments. The tips are great, but I think it is a mindset that you need to create if you are going to do it.

For example, if I have to travel for business in the school holidays, can one or more children or even my husband come with me?

I get asked to a lot of events that are important for me to attend, often with a 'plus one'. These days, that is just as likely to be CC#1 or even CC#2 as Mr M. Thus they have been to the ballet, the opera and the theatre – all the while supporting my career.

I have spoken at the world-renowned book festival in Hay-on-Wye, in Wales, in both 2010 and 2011, and both times took a Cost Centre with me. In 2011, on arrival in Hay with CC#3, I realized that I had forgotten to pack any school books for him and he had school exams the following week. He wasn't exactly unhappy about that – and anyway, as I pointed out to him, the Hay Festival is an education in itself.

First up, current affairs: a session where a panel were reviewing the daily papers. CC#3 is determined to go into the army, and was suitably thoughtful as they discussed a moving piece by *The Independent*'s sailing correspondent about losing his son in Afghanistan.

Next lesson, technology: I did a live online Q&A session for people who couldn't get to Hay to see me.

This was followed by mathematics – he had to figure out what change he would get from a ten-pound note when he bought a hot chocolate – and economics when we realized that I had been switched to a 430-seat auditorium from my original 100-seat venue.

After my event, we went to listen to Jonathan Stroud (CC#3 is a keen student of the Bartimaeus books) who gave us a creative writing, art and typography lesson. Then we had a science lesson in the Wiggly Worm corner (worms, soil and plants) before finishing up with drama, music and history when we watched a dramatic reading of *War Horse*.

I had replaced the school. Integrate or suffocate, indeed.

It's OK to be 'off duty' and call for backup

Finally, here are two suggestions for how to do it all, also both mentioned by Klein.

Make sure that you conserve your energy so that you can cope with having to do so many things. You will need time off to yourself. Klein calls this the 'Mom is off duty' solution – taking time out to recharge, and finding a way to do it so there are no interruptions.

In other words, your family must understand what 'off duty' means.

It sounds unbelievably selfish – and, once again, you will feel guilty taking time for yourself. But anything that restores your energy – from an hour asleep on a Saturday afternoon, right the way up to a two-day spa break with your girlfriend once a year – is well worth the investment.

Also, make sure you know who you can rely on as your backup. Klein highly recommends assembling a crisis team in advance of actually needing one. She describes it as a SWAT team, 'a personal group of special backup people' who fill in at home or at work when you have a real emergency. This may include neighbours, friends and relatives, and an arrangement needs to be reached for how to compensate them – in kind, or otherwise.

Life is unpredictable, so a SWAT team on standby can be a vital safety net – the 'Posse' Lynda Gratton describes (and which I mentioned in Chapter 2).

I have even known people move house and relocate to be nearer better backup.

It is well worth it.

In this chapter, I hope that I have explained one of the key challenges that face women, rather than men, on their way to the top. The reality is, they will have to pack a lot more into their days because they will still be the ones responsible for so much at home. And that will still be the case, even if their partner stays home to take care of things.

So, prioritize according to what is important for you, then outsource, be organized, speak up for what you need, conserve your energy, and be tolerant and patient when things are not done as well as you would have done them yourself.

This is the (relatively small) price that you will pay for a successful career.

Above all, remember that you *can* manage to do it all – one way or another – with help.

Theresa Ahlstrom, managing partner of KPMG LLP, and mother of two, put it better than I can: 'I always tell new mothers you can't give up after six months. It takes time to get all the pieces to fit together, but it will happen.'

At any stage of your career

Determine what in your life could be outsourced to free you up

Keep a diary for a week, recording everything you do with your time.

Now, review this and pick three things you could possibly outsource to others.

Think about what you could do if you had that extra time.

If you didn't have to clean the apartment, could you study for a part-time MBA?

Use lists to be more organized

When I fly a plane, I have a checklist of everything I need to do at every stage. I have it typed out and laminated, and I put multiple copies in the cockpit to make sure it is there. This approach is key for anything you do.

Are you going on holiday?

Write a list of what you need to take. It will save time.

Going grocery shopping?

Write a list of what you need. Then you can either order it online or go to the store – either way, it will be quicker.

Preparing for Christmas?

Have lists of everything – including food, and who to buy which presents for. I have a notebook and carry it around with me all the time, then use spare moments to check back through my lists and add to them.

Preserve your energy

Try these simple tips. You will be amazed at how much energy they preserve, and how much time they free up.

- Keep paper and pen by your bed in case you wake up and think of things you need to do. Otherwise, you will lie awake worrying about whether you will forget things in the morning.
- Free yourself from the tyranny of email. Put your BlackBerry in a drawer at the weekend and only take it out once a day for half an hour. Try doing that even during the week. Set aside a certain time of the day to review and answer your emails, rather than keeping a watching eye on them.

CHAPTER 7

FINANCIAL LITERACY

How good are you with numbers?

At some level, you need to have a grasp of them – and if you are really good with numbers, you probably have your career assured.

There are three reasons why I would encourage women to become as good with numbers as they can.

- Firstly, to be totally on top of your own personal finances, which frees you up to focus on your career.
- Secondly, to make sure you understand the language of the most senior people in business – what they call the 'C-suite'.
- And finally, and perhaps most critically, because most of the women at the top have been in charge of corporate money at some point.

Miranda Lane has a wonderful laugh, the infectious kind that makes you warm to her immediately. She lives in the countryside, loves horses, has a husband, two children and a great figure that she hides under a long line of black trouser suits that make her look smart and efficient when she walks into a room. She is particularly gifted at explaining things, telling stories, and making complex ideas simple to understand – which is just as well, because she runs a small but highly successful training company that she has built up from scratch over the last decade or so.

Miranda didn't start her career in training. Instead, she was herself trained – as a chartered accountant, qualifying in 1985 at Touche Ross. She had been to Exeter University and studied politics – not the obvious subject for someone who would then embark on a career based on numbers.

Why did she head in that direction?

She explained her reasons to me.

I decided to do accountancy because I had undershot everyone's expectations up to and including my degree due to lack of application and too much fun. I wanted a proper career and was thinking about investment banking so realized I needed to do something serious. I mentioned it to a rather pompous man who said, in effect, "Don't you bother your pretty little head with difficult stuff like accountancy," which was like the proverbial red rag. I immediately applied to be an accountant.

Not every woman in the world is motivated to become a qualified accountant. But if you want to aim for the top, I recommend you act on my three really important reasons why you need to know your numbers.

Know enough about money to know what is going on with your own

Ambitious women focus on what they do – the job in hand – but if they are not working with figures, their energy and effort will usually be directed away from the dollars and cents in their own life.

Take the example of Lady Gaga. When interviewed by Stephen Fry in the *Financial Times* in 2011, she gave an illustration of how completely dedicated she is to her career. She had appeared on a UK talk show, and Fry had assumed it would be no big deal for such an international superstar. But she had watched the programme afterwards, when it went to air.

❝ I watched it over and over and over and over and over. And I looked at all the parts that I liked and all the parts that I didn't like [. . .] and I said, "OK, maybe this part, if your breath control was different, and here, maybe you should try this step . . ." I study everything that I do to become better all the time at my craft. ❞

She went on to say:

❝ I'm not obsessed with material things and don't care about the money and don't care about the attention of the public, but only the love of my fans, so for me it's about how much more devoted, how much better an artist can I become. ❞

So, she focuses. That's great, and ambitious women should follow her example in that respect.

But not to the exclusion of financial awareness.

Note Lady Gaga's mention of her lack of regard for 'material things', which she makes sound like a virtue. It is not. The part of the interview that I remember most was when she described her approach to money in more detail, saying, 'It's honestly true that money means nothing to me.'

She disclosed that she was bankrupt after the first extension of The Monster Ball Tour.

‘ And it was funny because I didn't know! And I remember I called everybody and said, "Why is everyone saying I have no money? This is ridiculous, I have five Number One singles." And they said, "Well, you're $3 million in debt." ’

That didn't sound funny to me – ambitious women need to be on top of their finances. I think Lady Gaga realizes that now.

In March 2011, MasterCard launched its inaugural Index of Financial Literacy in Asia/Pacific/Middle East/Africa.

Do you know in which country in Asia/Pacific (including Australia and New Zealand) women came out on top?

Not Australia. Not Hong Kong, or Japan. But Thailand.

Thailand is much poorer than the other countries – this indicates that when women have to count every penny, they know where their money goes. With all the resources we have at our fingertips – whether we have only a modest income (at the moment) or multiple Number One hits under our belt – there is no excuse for not knowing how to get the most out of our money.

In 2006, as a senior at Harvard, Alexa von Tobel came up with the idea for LearnVest, a personal finance website for women. After realizing that there were no formal courses and only lacklustre resources for financial management for women, she founded a website that has now raised more than $5 million and educated many women.

Do you know everything about your own finances?

Do you have a spreadsheet somewhere with all your investments, or even all your debts, in one place?

Remember, mastering you own finances will set you free.

I feel especially strongly about this in marriage, or in a partnership of any kind.

Never, never go into a partnership – business or personal – with anyone if you do not know enough about the finances to ask the right questions.

I think every woman has her own personal boundaries in a marriage – ones which, if crossed, are taken very seriously. My own personal boundary is financial transparency. Mr M. can leave huge piles of clothes on the bedroom floor, retune all the radios in the house (and cars) to sports channels, and yet again fail to give me a present on our wedding anniversary, but any kind of secrecy about money will send me over the top. In my marriage that might be the purchase of a new and very expensive golf club. In another woman's it might be a secret bank account somewhere that her husband doesn't tell her about, or a reluctance to disclose his annual bonus.

That implies a lack of trust.

Being on top of your domestic finances is a very good start for any ambitious woman, married or not. On your way to achieving your career goals, you may need to take a career break, or retrain to acquire a new skill, or obtain experience of a particular industry (or with a particular company) to add to your CV. Some or all of this may require you to earn less money – and sometimes you may have to work for no money at all.

How will you know if this is possible, if you don't know how much you need to live on?

Your options will be so much greater if you try and minimize debt, and if you know where every penny goes – or is saved.

As a woman, you should be saving money. During the course of my career, I have taken advice from lots of people who I regard as mentors (even if they never formally took the title). Someone who greatly influenced my career once expressed surprise that I was not wealthier. It was true – I had reached the point of buying my company and had been forced to borrow every penny. Part of the reason was that I had spent eight years in banking without ever being paid properly (I was a trailing spouse for most of that time and, like many women, valued the flexibility I was shown more than the money), but mostly it was because I had never developed a serious savings habit.

When I go and talk in schools, I share this with young women and stress the importance of accumulating financial capital. Life expectancy, especially for women, is rocketing. We are all going to live longer than our mothers, and much longer than our grandmothers.

How are we going to be able to afford this, if we don't save money right from the start?

In the UK, two-thirds of pensioners who live in poverty are women. Given the high divorce rate in the UK, and the fact that over half of divorces occur when the woman is over forty-five years of age, it is essential to take control and build your own financial capital.

On the website Millionaire Mommy Next Door,

Jen Smith describes how she went from earning the minimum wage as a graveyard-shift waitress to financial freedom as a self-made millionaire by the age of forty. Jen bootstrapped half a dozen small businesses while working from home in her pyjamas. She learned how to invest in the stock market and in herself.

❝ Women need more money than men. Why? (No, not so we can buy more shoes, handbags and manicures.) We need more money because we live longer than men, make significantly less salary than our male peers, and are more likely to be single parents raising a family on one income. Women comprise 87 per cent of the impoverished elderly. A woman who works full-time for forty years will earn $523,000 less than her male counterpart. At age sixty-five, that extra half a million dollars could keep her from becoming one of the elderly poor! What do these grim statistics tell us? They tell us that women, especially as they become older, are not well prepared to take care of themselves financially. Yet nearly 90 per cent of all women will end up managing their finances alone at some point in their lives. ❞

Go out and buy a book on personal finance, such as *Love is Not Enough: The Smart Woman's Guide to Making (and Keeping) Money* written by Merryn Somerset Webb (aka My Cleverest Girlfriend).

It is worth investing a bit more of your time (and even money) in getting your head around a vital and increasingly complex subject. Economics Professor Annamaria Lusardi stressed how important it is for women to save for their retirement. She admits that she didn't follow her own advice and finds herself 'playing catch-up now, at the age of fifty, which is not a great place to be and certainly limits some of my options in life'.

Of course, savings are not only important for when you retire.

If you are married and planning a career break to have children, have you put aside some of your hard-earned money from your career to date into an account in your sole name?

Nothing will be more annoying than having to go cap in hand to your husband for cash every time you want to go to the hairdresser, or take your mother out to lunch. Those of you reading this at an early stage of your career, before you get married or have a career break, please don't underestimate how miserable this can make you feel. My Longest-Standing Girlfriend describes it as 'soul-destroying', even for a woman whose husband is happy for her to spend whatever she wishes to.

Having to ask for money affects your confidence, and gives you the feeling that you have lost your independence, which can be so discouraging.

If you think this obsession with finance is just the ranting of an overeducated, overweight woman with a fetish for accountants, I recommend you turn to the literature.

Financial literacy is very important. People with low financial literacy are:

- more likely to have problems with debt
- less likely to participate in the stock market
- less likely to choose mutual funds with lower fees

- less likely to accumulate wealth and manage wealth effectively
- less likely to plan for retirement.

In July 2010, according to the Insolvency Service, the number of British women going bankrupt had risen almost fivefold since 2000. It seems that younger women in particular were finding it difficult to manage their money, with those between the ages of 25 and 44 making up almost two-thirds of female bankruptcies. The long-standing women's organization the Fawcett Society says this is a feminist issue and the debt is caused by women typically earning less, owning less, and having a lower earning potential. Others say it is because women are being irresponsible with their money, and lack financial literacy.

It is probably both – but, most importantly, the two are intricately connected.

What's more, financial advisers believe that many women need to 'be prodded' to evaluate whether they're being paid what they're worth, because women 'simply aren't as confident and knowledgeable about financial matters as men'.

We need to become more confident, and more knowledgeable, and so I encourage you all to learn more about finance.

Start by making sure that you know everything about your own finances.

Do you know where every bank account is?

Do you know the outstanding balance of every credit card (and can order them from top to bottom in terms of the interest you pay on them)?

Do you have a plan to pay off your mortgage?

Good.

Learn the language of the people at the top of the career ladder

Now we can move on to the second reason why you need to improve your financial literacy – it is essential that you learn the language of the other people you will meet on your way up, and at the top of, the career ladder.

Money, as any student of economics knows, is a medium of exchange, a unit of account, and a store of value. It is the language by which the values of one world – a tonne of wheat, a barrel of oil – can be expressed in another – a motor car, a designer dress. Understanding money – at least, at what I would call a 'foundation' level – and what it pays for will give you the language that will enable you to talk to anyone about almost anything. Successful people all understand money, even if their success is not in the financial arena.

Madonna will know how much her gross ticket sales were on her last concert tour, down to the last dollar.

Melinda Gates will know how much a unit of polio vaccine costs.

Fiona Reynolds, who runs the National Trust in the UK – a member organization that receives no public subsidy and yet cares for the majority of our ancient buildings and much of our countryside – will know her annual budget and what her major revenue and cost centres are.

Whoever you work for, ask yourself some fundamental questions.

Do you know what the financial performance of your employer is?

Have you read its most recent annual report, including the notes – and do you understand most of it?

How does it compare to its competitors, and to its peers?

If it is a private company, it will still have filed accounts somewhere. If it is a not-for-profit, or a government department, it will have metrics on which its performance is judged. Do you know what they are – or do you know only about your little bit of the organization?

I counsel every ambitious woman to learn to read the *Financial Times*. You can get the *FT* everywhere these days, even in hard copy – but, if not, you could substitute whatever the business daily is in your country. Understanding whatever financial performance is being discussed – whether it is of companies or countries – will give you the language of the people at the top. And you do have to learn to read these papers; it is not like picking up *Hello!* magazine. I had to learn to read the *FT* as a student, and I try to teach all my employees to do so too. At first glance it is an impenetrable paper but, if you learn to read it piece by piece, you will realize that there are many parts of it that are highly readable – even for someone who is a beginner.

When you read the *FT* regularly, you join the most exclusive club in the world – the club whose members are the people who matter, the people who breathe the air that you want to breathe, who turn left on the plane (or have their own), who control the companies and countries that really make things happen. Even when I have read the whole paper on the Internet, I still buy and carry a paper copy whenever I can, and especially when I travel. It makes a statement about me, about my newspaper of choice, that says: 'I am a grown-up who is worth speaking to, even if you're one of the most important and influential people in the world.'

Acquire financial literacy as a route to the top

Let's assume you are totally on top of your own finances and read the *FT* regularly. You can discuss XYZ company's decision to waive their dividend, or the collapse of the Irish bubble economy, with anyone you meet in the business-class (or, hopefully, first-class) lounge.

But that may not be enough to get to the top.

The third, and perhaps most compelling, reason to become financially literate is that finance is a proven route to the top. If you are reading this book and want to run a major organization one day – and especially if you want to be in charge of a large publicly quoted company – I urge you to seek a formal financial qualification.

One woman with an extremely high-profile plural career, as cited by the Cranfield 'Female FTSE Index', is Alison Carnwath. Aspirant women can take heart: Alison didn't go to Oxford or Cambridge, but to the reassuringly redbrick University of Reading. And she does not have an MBA. However, Alison did qualify as a chartered accountant with Peat Marwick Mitchell, becoming an investment banker in 1980. She spent twenty years building that part of her career before resigning to take up directorships that currently include the chairmanship of Land Securities, Barclays and Man Group – all FTSE 100 constituents. Her ACA helped to set her up for the big league.

Elsewhere, the same pattern emerges.

Many of the women playing a role on supervisory boards of companies in the FTSE Eurofirst 300 have finance backgrounds and/or qualifications, and quite a few have legal qualifications, which is another excellent building block for a successful career.

When PepsiCo named Indian-born Indra Nooyi, who still routinely wears a sari and who used to front an all-female rock band, as its chief executive designate in August 2006, it was always going to draw comment. 'Ms Nooyi will become the world's most important female chief executive,' said *The Economist*.

Not much was written, though, about her chosen route to the top. Before she became chief executive, Indra was the president and CFO of Pepsi – and this despite the fact that she is not a professional accountant. Her undergraduate degree, from Madras Christian College in India, was in chemistry, physics and mathematics; she earned a master's in finance and marketing from the Indian Institute of Management in Calcutta; and she also holds a master's in public and private management from the Yale School of Management. Her progress to the boardroom of PepsiCo was via several other positions (including at Asea Brown Boveri and Motorola, on whose board she still sits) and a stint in management consultancy.

It would be a strong bet to say that, when making their decision about Indra, the directors of PepsiCo would have been favourably impressed by her knowledge of the company and her ability to understand its every facet: her previous job was described by Business Round-table as being responsible for 'PepsiCo's corporate functions, including finance, strategy, business process optimization, corporate platforms and innovation, pro-curement, investor relations and information technology'.

Being the CFO was very helpful to Indra – she had visibility of the whole business, and became very visible herself.

Many other women have gone down that same route on their way to the top.

When she became the finance director of Lloyds TSB, Helen Weir was arguably Britain's most powerful female CFO. (Yes, we have returned to Helen – it's worth understanding how you can build your career to earning more than £1 million a year.) Like Indra, she has an undergraduate degree in mathematics and a postgraduate degree in management, plus, as we men-tioned earlier, a management accountancy qualification from her time at Unilever. All of which no doubt helps when you are managing the finances of a bank capital-ized at £30 billion. In another striking similarity to the new PepsiCo chief executive, Helen spent her early car-eer in management consultancy, with McKinsey. In 2006, she won the *Harper's Bazaar*/Chanel Business-woman of the Year Award, an honour bestowed on women who have made it up the corporate ladder and reached the highest echelons of business life.

In the four preceding years, the winners had all owned strong financial pedigrees. Bibiana Boerio, in 2011 the finance and strategy director for Ford's International Operations, was managing director of Jaguar when she won. She is a long-serving Ford staff member, and has held several finance positions, including executive vice-president and CFO of Ford Credit, as well as previously being parachuted into Jaguar as director of finance when it was first acquired by Ford.

See? It helps to do a finance job on the way to the top.

Another previous winner of the award was Vivienne Cox, then executive vice-president of a division of BP that, had it been separately listed, would have been a FTSE 100 constituent in its own right. She was at the time the only female member of BP's executive committee. Her undergraduate degree (like Helen's, from Oxford, and, like part of Indra's, in chemistry) was followed by a master's in the same subject. It led her to BP, where she moved into its finance function very early on, becoming part of the team that masterminded the privatization of the company. Yet another example of finance being a route to the top of the biggest companies.

Given that this is all so well documented, why don't more ambitious women choose this path?

Jeremy Rickman of Russell Reynolds Associates is a respected headhunter based in Chicago who specializes in finding talented CFOs for some of the world's most successful companies. Jeremy, himself a chartered accountant and former finance director, says that the quality of the female candidates he sees keeps rising. 'More and more women are making their mark as finance directors, and I would expect this to continue,' he told me. Russell Reynolds Associates also searches for chief executives, and Jeremy is well aware that the financial officers he finds today are increasingly expected to provide succession options for the top job in the future.

Helen endorses the view that a professional qualification will aid ambitious women.

> Every senior manager I know is very comfortable with numbers – they can look at a profit and loss account or balance sheet and understand what it's saying. Having that capability is a very important prerequisite for making it to the top of a business. Not all executives have a professional finance qualification, but I think it's a great place to start.

Of course, not every woman who ends up as the chief executive of a public company has started life as an accountant, and some of them have deliberately chosen not to take that route. Belinda Earl, who was appointed chief executive of Debenhams at the age of thirty-eight and is now the chief executive of Jaeger and Aquascutum, studied economics at university but turned down a training contract at Arthur Andersen in order to take up a place on the Harrods graduate training scheme instead. Two years later, in 1985, she moved to Debenhams, working her way up through the ranks to take charge of merchandising and trading – and, finally, the whole company.

It's good to know that there are other ways in, but I am interested that she was offered an accountancy training contract, even though she did not take it. It shows that she had the aptitude for figures, even at a young age. She has also previously stressed the importance of a good grounding in finance.

⟨ I would encourage individuals who are keen to climb the corporate ladder to gain not only an appreciation of, but really a full grounding in finance, not just the standard balance sheet, or profit and loss, but a complete awareness of business levers. Retailing, from running a store through to buying and merchandising a product area, requires all of these skills. ⟩

Are you getting the point here?

Women at the top are financially literate. And usually have the qualifications to match.

Avon is one of the most successful cosmetics companies in the world. In November 2011, it appointed a female CFO, Kimberly Ross, who had spent the previous decade with the giant Dutch retailer Ahold. In that time she had held various senior positions in treasury, tax and finance, and eventually became CFO and a member of the Corporate Executive Board in November 2007. When her departure from Ahold was announced, her CEO at Ahold, Dick Boer, praised her contribution to the company and credited her for Ahold becoming 'a stable and financially sound company with a strong balance sheet'.

Kimberly is not a chartered accountant, but she did get a BA in accounting from the University of South Florida. She then started her career in internal audit at Anchor Glass. Internal audit is not often considered a sexy career choice, but it does allow you to see every part of the inside of a company and how it works – better training, almost, than any MBA.

I often advise people who are determined to break into investment banking but are finding it hard to win a seat in the mergers and acquisitions department to try for internal audit. It is a great way into any organization.

Of course, finance is not the only way to the top. Law, which is another well-understood professional qualification that appears on the CVs of many very senior men, is another route. Successful women as varied as Marjorie Scardino (CEO of Pearson plc, the ultimate owner of the publisher of this book), Amelia Fawcett (chair of the *Guardian* Media Group), Maria da Cunha (general counsel, British Airways) and Sara Geater (CEO of TV production company Talkback Thames) all have a legal background. Even when we look back to the winner of the inaugural *Harper's* Award, Sian Westerman, she was a law graduate from Birmingham University who qualified as a solicitor with Slaughter and May before changing career and becoming the first female investment banker in Rothschild's London office.

But accountancy is a far more certain route.

In 2011, Catalyst (a not-for-profit membership organization that is dedicated to expanding the opportunities for women in business) published some figures about women working in finance in the USA. Here (in italics) is what I thought of the headlines.

- Women are 60.1 per cent of all accountants and auditors. *That's great!*
- In a 2009 study, women were 55 per cent of newly hired accounting graduates, and 41 per cent of all CPAs. *That's also pretty encouraging.*
- Women are 23 per cent of all partners at firms, although they are 49 per cent of all accounting

employees at accounting firms. *That's rather less encouraging.*

In a 2010 study, examining the number of women partners at the Big Four accounting firms in 2009, women were 18.1 per cent of all equity partners at the Big Four. *That is just not good enough.*

The proportion of female members of six major chartered accountancy bodies worldwide inched up from 22 per cent in 1999 to 33 per cent in 2009, according to the Financial Reporting Council. But the number of female students has remained constant (except for 2008) since 2004, at 48 per cent – although, between 2004 and 2009, the percentage of female students at the Institute of Chartered Accountants for England and Wales actually fell by 3 per cent.

Given that we know that finance and financial literacy is the route to the top, we need more accountants.

Please encourage every young woman you know to go out and qualify. Stop them from applying direct from their undergraduate degree to Wall Street – they can go and qualify first, and Wall Street will still welcome them. In fact, it will welcome them more.

My top tip for qualifying is to do so in a city where you will have really interesting clients to work with. In the UK, for instance, I often encourage young women to qualify in Birmingham or Bristol, rather than London, so that they are auditing companies of a more manageable size and can get to see how these companies operate.

In the USA, a Certified Public Accountant (CPA) is the statutory title of qualified accountants who have passed the Uniform Certified Public Accountant Examination. The criteria for eligibility to sit the exam vary slightly from one state to another, but usually require approximately 150 semester hours if you don't have an accountancy degree.

But did you know that you can also sit for the Uniform CPA Examination outside the USA – including in Japan, Bahrain, Kuwait, Lebanon and the United Arab Emirates?

Once you have passed the exam, you need to gain relevant experience – usually one to two years – before you can practise.

And me?

As I mentioned earlier in this book, I didn't qualify as an accountant. I don't 'do' regret – like guilt, I think it is a wasted use of emotional energy. But the one thing I almost regret is that I never became a chartered accountant. So, as I said in Chapter 3, I am planning to do my management accountancy exams as a way of marking my fiftieth birthday, the year that this book is published.

If you meet me, ask me how I am getting on.

I did management accounting as part of my MBA at the London Business School, taught by Andrew Liekerman who is now the Dean – and I am sure that is why I see my children as cost centres.

But it would be valuable to have the letters after my name.

Finally, one more word on Miranda Lane (one of the many objects of my accountant envy). Her training company is called Finance Talking, and it trains people all over the world to understand the language of the

capital markets and the metrics of financial performance, and to be able to communicate them.

You may not want to be an accountant, but the reason why Miranda's company has been so successful is
because so many people realize that, in order to advance
in their careers, they need her and her team to teach
them to understand the numbers. My hope is that many
more of her clients in the future will be women. It will
be a sign that more women are on their way to the top.

I hope I have demonstrated how financial literacy is
an important skill for ambitious women. At the very
least, please master your own finances, because it will
open up more options for you in the future.

The best and most certain route to the top is by
acquiring a formal finance qualification. This will not be
for everyone – but, for those of us able to obtain one,
it is probably the quickest way to career success.

How to become more financially literate

Get on top of your own finances

Do a spreadsheet with a list of all your debts (mortgage, credit cards, overdraft, student loans and even loans from family members) and a list of all the interest rates you are paying.

Update it on the first of the month, or whenever you get the statements.

Keep on the same spreadsheet all the assets you may have (property, savings) and what they are worth.

Are you building assets?

Or are you increasing your liabilities?

Get your income and outgoings more in balance so that you can save – however little, at first.

What might this take – cost cutting, or getting a second job?

Work out what your financial targets should be

Work out what your own personal 'financial finish line' is.

At the London Business School TEDx event in May 2011, Payal Patel made the case strongly for working out exactly how much money is 'enough'.

I, for instance, know I wish to be totally debt free, own three specific properties outright, and save an additional (and specific) sum into my pension fund, before I retire. I know what the exact figure is. As soon as I reach it, I will move to a plural career, giving more time to my 'third dimension' activities.

Do you know what your 'financial finish line' is?

Learn the language of the people at the top

Learn to read the *Financial Times*, and *The Economist*

Here's a quick way to do both – and remember, for both publications it is much cheaper to subscribe to them.

- *Financial Times*: Start by reading the digestible bits for four weeks. An example is Lucy Kellaway in the *FT* on a Monday, and one piece in the Lex column each day. Also, read the summaries on the left-hand side of the front pages of both sections. Then, for the next four weeks, add one more article each day. Try a new columnist each week, as well. John Kay, or Tim Harford, Andrew Hill or Michael Skapinker all write on management or economics. Learn to read Gillian Tett's work by starting with her more accessible column on a Saturday and then her harder-hitting, more technical finance articles. Register for the *FT* online and set up alerts for companies you are interested in – your employer, or that of your boyfriend/parent/partner.
- *The Economist*: Start by reading the summary pages 'The Week in Politics' and 'The Week in Business'. Then go through the index and pick out two articles a week that you would like to read, plus one book review, and the obituary (they only have one each issue).

Pick a company each month to study

Read its annual report (all public companies will post these on their website). Then try to find someone who works there, and ask them about it.

Do a Finance Talking course

Miranda's courses look at how companies are analysed and judged by third parties, and how companies communicate their financial performance. They are excellent introductions to how the financial markets operate, and she has both US and UK versions. But even more usefully, you can do the courses as e-learning, wherever you are. Visit http://www.financetalking.com – and if you don't know which to pick, email her and ask her! – miranda@financetalking.com.

Hasten your route to the top

Qualify as an accountant

It doesn't really matter what kind of accountant (management accounts or statutory accounts). And remember, some qualifications can be studied for part-time.

Consider doing your CFA

See Chapter 1 for the reasons why the CFA (Chartered Financial Analyst) is such a useful financial qualification – http://www.cfainstitute.org.

CHAPTER 8

THE THIRD
DIMENSION

It is not enough, I am afraid, to be good at your job. Or even to be good at your job and run your home life well.

To be truly successful, you need a third dimension to your life. And you need to plan and execute it well.

Why?

Because a third dimension to your life will make you more interesting and attractive as an employee – and, once you advance to more senior levels, can help you gain management and board experience too. Plus it can help you build your network (which, as we saw in Chapter 2, is very important).

I realized this after looking around at the successful women I know and admire, and also at those in the earlier stages of their careers on the way to the top. One of them is Helena Morrissey, who we met in Chapter 6. Helena has an unusual beauty. Slender, with pale, luminous skin and dark-brown eyes, she looks like the kind of woman that great artists might want to paint. If you are a young artist in the UK today, you have reason to be grateful to Helena, who sits on the board of the Royal Academy of Arts.

In April 2011, she brokered a three-year deal between her employer (the Bank of New York Mellon) and the RA to sponsor the RA Schools, which have been an integral part of the RA since their foundation in 1768. The deal will provide subsidies for students in cases of financial hardship. As Helena said, 'The role of the Royal Academy Schools is invaluable in nurturing the talent and ideas of young artists so as to safeguard the future of art.'

Helena has been a committed supporter of the RA for many years. But this is not the only thing that occupies her spare time. In November 2010, she set up the 30% Club, a campaigning group that hopes to raise the percentage of female representation on boards and in the senior ranks of public companies to 30 per cent by 2015.

In an interview in December 2010, she talked about:

> women's tendency not to push ourselves forward, and not working the political side of things [. . .] We need to get out there a bit more, shout a bit more loudly.

I hope I am helping her do the shouting – I sit on the steering committee of the 30% Club.

Her work with the RA and her founding of the 30% Club are the twin reasons why Helena's name is at the top of this chapter. I want to encourage all women to find that third dimension – an element of their lives that is not work, and not home.

If you are ambitious to succeed in your career, a third dimension will be critical. It can – and, indeed, at some level should – tie in with your interests either at work or at home, but it can also be something substantially different.

When you meet Helena, you realize she is not doing all this in an attempt at self-promotion; she is genuinely motivated to support worthy causes such as the RA, and to make a difference in the world through the 30% Club. But even if you don't have a philanthropic bone in your body, you need to develop a third dimension to your life.

Remember, in Chapter 2 I stressed the importance of building relationships with people who matter. In order to do that, you have to approach relationships from two angles.

- *Be interested in people.* I am hoping that you are socially skilled enough to be interested in other people – but, if not, please learn to be. Finding common ground with others will generate a genuine connection, rooted in mutual interests. Ask questions – make sure they are good ones, and have them ready in advance if you know you are going to meet someone for the first time. Show an interest in them, their business, their career, their family, their hobbies. If the conversation grinds to a halt, ask them something that will start them chatting again. American writer Dale Carnegie once said: 'To be interesting to other people, you have to be interested in them first.'
- *Be interesting to people.* Make sure you are interesting yourself. To do this, you need to find what I call a 'third dimension' to your life. This should be something that is not your main source of employment, or your family. Find something that you can engage in and make a meaningful contribution to, not something where you hover at the periphery.

Go the extra mile to have more to say

It is sometimes assumed – or inferred – that successful people will be involved in not-for-profit activities in order to 'give something back'. But I think it is unlikely that you will be successful in the first place unless you get involved with something outside of home and family.

When you are seated next to someone influential at dinner, when you meet them on an aeroplane, when you are interviewed for a job, it will be the third dimension in your life that will help you stand out, be memorable, get them interested in you. If you have a very unusual or exotic job, maybe it will be enough (although, if you're a pole dancer or an FBI undercover agent, you may not want to mention your job), but I put it to you that your source of employment may not be enough to sustain a conversation of any length or interest to someone senior. This is especially true early on in your career.

Your family may be a key part of your life, but it is not usually a good topic for conversation. In fact, as you get older and have children, conversation about your family could be downright boring. Not many senior businessmen, or even businesswomen, want to get stuck next to someone whose only conversation is about the limited confines of a narrow job and/or whether organic baby food is worth the extra money.

At the start of your career, when you are applying for college, the third dimension is critical, and it remains so throughout your career. There's a reason why universities ask for evidence of a 'third dimension'. Top grades only tell you so much about a person – they're not enough to make you stand out. Barry Taylor, director of communications at the University of Bristol, says:

If you want to study English at a leading university, you will need to have discovered some favourite authors and have some ideas about these authors. You may well be so *committed* [author's emphasis] you may run a book club, or have written some material of your own. 〞

To illustrate how the unconventional and the unusual (as well as the personal) sticks in people's minds, look at the list below.

1. Interest rates
2. Voluntary work with victims of human trafficking
3. The royal wedding
4. US foreign policy
5. Climate change

Close your eyes for twenty seconds, then open them and recite the list.

Chances are, you remembered the human-trafficking voluntary work.

Your third dimension doesn't have to be charitable. It could be sport: I know a very successful woman who played excellent hockey to a very high standard all the way to the age of forty; and a woman in her twenties who is a killer poker player and regularly uses her vacation to work the tournament circuit. Sport is a very acceptable third dimension – if you can play it to a high enough level, or get involved with it administratively.

Lucy Pearson, who will be forty years old in 2012, is the inspirational head of a thriving mixed-sex secondary school outside Manchester, Cheadle Hume School. She started there in the summer of 2010. It is her first headship, although she has held senior positions in two other prominent schools before this one. She is a graduate of Oxford University and, I am reliably told by Cost

Centre #1, she is a pretty impressive English teacher. But less than a third of her 244-word Wikipedia entry is devoted to her teaching career, because she played cricket for the England women's team and is a world record holder for her performance against the Australians in 2003 where she took eleven wickets in a single Test Match. That 'third dimension' will have featured in every job interview she has ever had, and taught her so much about leadership and team work.

I am sure she would have risen to great heights as a teacher and a head without ever playing cricket – but I am equally sure that having done so will have helped her stand out from the crowd when her teaching career was in its infancy.

Are you keen on a sport, but not good enough to play it to a high standard?

Become an umpire. Manage a team. (It is not really enough to turn out for the local pub soccer team once a month, or occasionally put the TV on to watch the tennis – that won't make you interesting enough.)

Tellingly, this third dimension is something that employers as well as colleges appear to understand the value of. I gave a talk on the subject at the London Business School Women in Business Conference, and my audience reported that the third dimension is something they are increasingly getting questions about in interviews for jobs.

Please don't try to say that your job doesn't leave you enough time.

Remember Helena, who I described at the start of this chapter?

She is the CEO of Newton, BNY Mellon's UK-based global equity and multi-asset specialist, which has £50 billion under management. She became CEO in 1994 at the age of thirty-five. Just for good measure, she is a director of the UK's Investment Management Association – a trade body – and represents the fund management industry on the Financial Services Authority's Practitioner Panel.

And she still manages to do work with the RA and the 30% Club.

So, what is your excuse?

If you are thinking about using your home life as an excuse instead, that won't wash either. Helena has no fewer than nine children. I feel exhausted even writing that. You might be amazed to hear that this is with the one husband – but what is even more impressive is that she has achieved this while using the services of the same nanny throughout. She admits that her home is run 'like a military operation', and she is lucky enough to have the support of a stay-at-home husband – but even so, finding time for a third dimension must be challenging.

Be a giver rather than a taker

Do you think that you are already very interesting?

Good!

But even if you are, there is another reason why you might find it useful to develop a third dimension to your life. It will help you to build your own regenerative network (which I advocated in Chapter 2). Take a look at the people who sit on the boards of not-for-profit organizations. On the whole, they are people who anyone would be interested to meet and to count among their circle of acquaintances and advocates.

When you are building a network, it is important to be a giver rather than a taker, as I stressed in Chapter 2.

Young people early on in their career often ask me how they can possibly have anything to offer older, more senior and successful people after they meet them and want to continue the relationship. I would recommend that you find out what their third dimension is (if you haven't already researched this even before meeting them) and then offer to assist with it.

At the very least, you can offer to be a volunteer at a fund-raising event.

When I meet someone who impresses me, and I decide I would like to spend more time with them and ultimately count them as an acquaintance, I ask myself, 'What can I do for them?' Even if you are just out of college, that is the mindset you should adopt.

Have you won a global piano competition?

Sailed solo round the world?

Made your first million by the age of twenty-one?

Even if you are already terribly interesting, and already have a brilliant network of friends and advocates, helping somebody you have met with their third dimension is a very good way to go about doing something for them – giving, rather than taking.

Use your third dimension to get on board

There is another reason, particularly if you are a woman, to adopt a third dimension to your life, and to pursue it to the top.

We need more women on the boards of, and acting as trustees for, not-for-profit organizations. Joining the board of a not-for-profit will give you the skills and experience required in the boardroom. This involves advising rather than doing, and advising in a consensual way. Not-for-profit boards, especially the bigger ones, operate just like the boards of commercial, publicly listed companies – they have committees, they have to identify and secure new trustees, they have to elect chairmen, appoint CEOs.

All of that experience will stand you in very good stead when it comes to getting a job in the board-room of a commercial company. You will gain the skills, but also the confidence, to aim for a board position within your own company. Or any other company for that matter.

And boy, do we need more women on the boards of companies.

In the UK, approximately 12 per cent of the people on the boards of the top 100 public companies are women – and if you exclude the non-executive direct-ors, it is more like 6 per cent. In the USA, representation of women on the boards of Standard & Poor's 500 companies was 16 per cent in 2011, according to the Bloomberg Rankings annual analysis.

In the UK, this is why Helena founded the 30% Club. She is using her position as the CEO of a fund manager, and therefore a major institutional shareholder, to lobby for change. She says:

❛ I realize that you do have a bit of responsibility if you have achieved a certain position and can then use it effectively. I know Newton isn't the hugest company, but we do run £50 billion of money. We have a lot of relationships, a lot of pension funds and clients, and I am involved in broader industry things. And if that means that people will talk to me, then I should be prepared to talk about it. ❜

Neither Helena nor I are fans of quotas. They were introduced in Norway, and now that country has the highest proportion of female company directors in Europe, so they appear, at first sight, to be the answer. However, none of the data that has been published since shows any improved performance by Norwegian companies. Fans of quotas argue that they help to increase the number of women who are qualified to sit on boards by making sure there are more women with experience. Personally, I think they lead to 'token' appointments. There is a website that lists all the women appointed to FTSE 100 and 250 boards every year, and the great thing is that every woman on the list has been appointed for her own skills and experience, not because the chairman had to fill a government quota.

It is helpful, if you want to get more women on boards, to have chairmen who actively support increased representation, and this is what Helena and the rest of us in the 30% Club are actively seeking to achieve. But that won't, of itself, be enough. We also need a lot more women who are board-ready.

How to get board-ready?

For a start, read and follow the advice in this book. And crucially, join the board of a not-for-profit – especially one that has other people on it who are already directors of public companies. This will give you useful board experience, and also improve your profile, both of which will help you be board-ready.

Other aspects of your third dimension then come into play. One book on this subject talks about the need to 'bring all of yourself to the table', meaning that building relationships with others through the discussion of non-business matters can really help you – and you can learn to do this by practising in the boardroom of a not-for-profit organization. This builds trust and facilitates empathy, as you're sharing much more of yourself than just your views on the business matter in hand. The more interesting you are, the easier this will be to achieve. Don't forget to arm yourself with topics other than family and work.

It helps to have government encouragement, of course. In the UK, the Davies Report was published in 2011, calling for boards to have at least 25 per cent women by 2015. The report calls on the Financial Reporting Council (FRC) to amend the UK Corporate Governance Code so that it requires listed companies to:

establish a policy concerning boardroom diversity, including measurable objectives for implementing the policy, and disclose annually a summary of the policy and the progress made in achieving the objectives.

At the time of writing, the jury is still out on whether

the FRC will amend its code, although the FRC does acknowledge that a lack of women on boards:

may weaken the board by encouraging 'group think' [...] may demonstrate a failure to make full use of the talent pool [... and may result in] weak [...] connectivity with, or understanding of, customers and workforce and offer little encouragement to aspiration among female employees.

This encouragement, plus the requirement to disclose their targets and the progress made towards meeting them, is, in my view, much better than quotas, which I am resolutely opposed to. Personally, I don't aspire to sit on a public company board – I can meet all my career goals and objectives without doing so, and I don't much fancy the legal and financial responsibilities that come with such an appointment. I have enough of those in my own business, and at home.

But I am keen to see more women on boards because I think both of them (the women and the boards) will benefit hugely.

At EU level, the European Commission launched a 'Strategy for Equality between Women and Men 2010–2015' in September 2010. As part of this strategy the Justice Commissioner, Viviane Reding, has asked all companies to pledge to have at least 30 per cent female board members by 2015, and 40 per cent by 2020.

In the USA, I think you need a 30% Club of your own. Maybe someone reading this book could start one?

And why are there no US government initiatives either?

A study by Corporate Women Directors International shows that the USA even lags behind countries such as

Bulgaria, Latvia and South Africa in the statistics for board representation by women. The only ray of light is that some corporations (including American Express, Cisco, Deloitte, Morgan Stanley and Intel) are experimenting with initiatives to give high-performing women the skills and support to move into leadership positions.

Professor Susan Vinnicombe of Cranfield School of Management has made a speciality of research into board diversity: each year her unit publishes a report on the number of women in the boardrooms of the UK's top 100 companies. (Bet she has no shortage of conversation with anyone.) She has reported some improvement, but not much. This may end up being an issue in itself. If things do not get better on either side of the Atlantic we may well end up with quotas – which will almost certainly lead to women being appointed just to make up the numbers, rather than on merit. That may well mean substandard women in the job. This won't help the male attitude, or provide the right role models.

Most shareholders could not care less if a company in which they have invested appoints a man, a woman or a Martian as its next non-executive director. What they want is for that non-exec to add value in terms of monitoring company performance, strategy and risk on behalf of the shareholders, and supporting the executive directors to achieve the highest possible return on capital employed. So, if you are a woman who wants to be in the boardroom, go and get experience of monitoring performance, strategy and risk – and getting it both in your day job and on the board of a not-for-profit is a great idea.

We will get an increasing number of women in the boardroom, not just from supply-side initiatives, but also from women sticking with their careers and building valuable experience, as did the late and much-admired Dame Hilary Cropper. Hilary was chair of Xansa, the computer group which started life as an all-women company. She was also a powerful advocate for equal opportunities, but she never made an issue of gender in her own career: she got there on merit.

And so, eventually, will many other people who are not white, not male and have never played golf with the chairman.

As the sixteen-page natty brochure *Brighter Boards for a Brighter Future*, published by the UK's Department of Trade and Industry in 2004, said:

You're in for the long haul. You may not be recruited immediately, but don't give up. Keep acquiring the skills that will one day take you into the boardroom where you know you belong.

How to add a third dimension to your life

It can be hard to add a third dimension to your life. This is especially true if you are at a very early stage of your career.

Here are some useful tips to get you started.

Make sure that you don't stand out for what you don't know

Everyone should know a little bit about a range of things. We should all know something about the classics – art, music, literature. We should all have a general understanding of history and politics.

We should all be aware of current events. I find compendiums very useful for this, especially when I am time-poor. At the very least, each week I read the following:

- the *Economist*'s summary pages ('The Week in Business' and 'The Week in Politics')
- the *Spectator*'s round-up of the week, and
- the front page of the BBC website (which I try to do daily).

Inspire people and infect them with some enthusiasm

But even assuming that you are reasonably well read, you still need a specific third dimension that sets your life apart from everyone else's. It should be something, ideally, that you are genuinely interested in, as well as it being good for your career.

In an interview with Oprah Winfrey in 2009, Maya Angelou said: 'I've learned that people will forget what you said, people will forget what you did, but people will never forget how you made them feel.'

A good starting point is to devise a checklist before you select what to spend your valuable time on outside your job and your home life. Here is mine.

- Is it something I feel passionate about? (Standing out involves not just being able to talk, competently, about a new interest – it depends on you drawing excitement, real interest, vitality and confidence from

it too. This will shine through when you discuss your
new adventure.)

▨ Does it fit well with my day job? (I would think hard,
for instance, before volunteering for Amnesty International if I worked for a company that manufac-
tured weapons.)

▨ Will it offer me the chance to bring genuine added
value to the organization?

▨ Will it offer me the right public profile (see Chapter 9)?

Back in 2000, I ran that checklist over an organization
called Tomorrow's People, who work with the long-term
unemployed. I do feel passionately about social exclusion, and about raising people's aspirations (especially
women's) and building their confidence so that they are
able to find a job and contribute positively to the economy. Employment was a sector that fitted well with my
day job, and so for the first year I volunteered one afternoon a fortnight at a counselling centre in south London,
adding (I hope) genuine value.

I worked my way from volunteer to the development
committee, and eventually to the board of trustees –
which, in turn, led me to meet many of the major
corporate funders of the organization and thus enabled
me to build my profile.

I have given lots of time and even, later on, money to
the organization, and brought my contacts as well, but
I would be the first to thank them for the support my
involvement with Tomorrow's People gave to my career.

How did I even find Tomorrow's People?

I asked someone I knew and respected about where
I should offer my time and energy, and told her that my

general interest lay in working with charities in the UK (there are many deserving causes abroad, but I thought I would start at home) and in social exclusion, rather than medical areas.

I would strongly advise you to seek a third dimension in the same way as you would seek a new job – or even a new boyfriend.

Ask people you trust to suggest something they think you would like.

Look at the bigger picture

When you do find something, think about how it fits into a bigger picture of, for example:

- national cultural importance
- environmental significance, or
- the international arena.

There is always a bigger picture. Know what the wider significance of your interest is and who the big players – both organizations and individuals – are.

Let me give you an example.

Are you interested in art?

Do you know which artworks are under threat from export, why, and what is going to be done to save them?

Do you know what is being sold at auction, and for what price?

Knowing the answers to these questions could make you very interesting indeed.

There are lots of arts organizations you can volunteer for. Look at the boards of all the great art institutions – most successful/influential people have an interest in art and culture. The Museum of Modern Art in New York, for instance, sports no fewer than three Rockefellers on its board. In the UK, the trustees of the Tate Gallery include Elisabeth Murdoch and Lionel Barber, the editor of the *Financial Times*.

The bigger picture is always useful.

Early on in your career, if you focus on being interesting and interested, the opportunities will be there – to serve in the areas of sport, the environment, education, health, and many other organizations and arenas. Start with offering your time and organizational abilities – no one expects a young person to have lots of money. Bringing your human capital – your skills – will be just as important. All charities and not-for-profit organizations need financial skills, legal skills, human resources skills. You can be sure that your skills and experience, if you have invested in your human capital, will be welcomed.

Bringing your social capital will be just as valuable. Long before you are able to write any meaningful cheque yourself, you might be able to invite people who can to a fund-raising event.

One of the most useful things you can do, even at a relatively early stage in your career, is to volunteer as the governor of a school. Even in a small primary school there will be issues with management, resource allocation, personality issues, and so on. These will serve as valuable training for later on – and, in the meantime, you will be bringing your own resources to a school that needs them.

This chapter has been all about doing voluntary work in order to further your career.

You may find that rather mercenary.

Surely, most people who volunteer do so for the good of the organization they serve and the people that it benefits?

Of course they do.

But they will have thought carefully about how and what they give their time and energies to – so that it supports their career, and vice versa.

Helena Morrissey's work with the Royal Academy, and the sponsorship her company gives, allows her to entertain Newton's clients at events to which they would never normally gain access. So, her efforts work for both the RA and her employer.

Finding a third dimension that benefits you, your career, your business or your family in some way at the same time as you are able to volunteer your skills creates a virtuous circle from which everyone profits.

I have explained how developing a third dimension to your life will help you to become more interesting, to develop your network further and, finally, will help you to acquire skills and experience that will serve your career well. But if you really want to help people less fortunate than yourself, you should read this book and focus on your career – and I mean every aspect of it, not just the charitable areas.

Why?

Because the best way to help the poor is to ensure you don't become one of them.

At the start of your career

How to think strategically about ways to develop a third dimension

Write down the things that interest you in all sorts of areas: sport, art, medical research, social issues. These are all potential third dimensions.

Now, pick one and research the organizations that are involved with it.

Do they have a national as well as a local presence?

Even if the answer is no, go and volunteer your time – and make it as much of a commitment as cleaning your teeth or going to the gym. (In fact, forget the gym. Every time I make a commitment to go to the gym, I fail to keep it.)

Do you want to serve your education community?

Look into becoming a school governor – in the UK, see the dedicated website http://www.sgoss.org.uk/home/.

Mid career

Review all the third-dimension activities you are involved with

If you are not involved with any, see the first homework assignment above.

Do you have more than two?

If so, you need to prioritize. Review all your personal

goals and priorities and match your third-dimension activities against them. Ideally, you should only have three at the most:

- one that you spend a lot of time on, your 'main' third dimension
- one that you spend some time on, and
- one that you spend almost no time on at all.

Anything beyond that, and you are almost certainly doing too much – unless you have a large staff you can delegate to.

Less than ten years to retirement

Make your third dimension your future career

If you had enough money to retire on, what third-dimension activity would you like to spend more time on?

Are there part-time or voluntary jobs in that area?

Do you need any special qualifications or experience to get those jobs? (For example, if it involves working with children in the UK, you will need special clearance.)

Now is the time to think about getting them.

CHAPTER 9

DOING YOUR OWN PR

Every woman should spend 5 per cent of her time doing her own PR.

'For most of history "Anonymous" was a woman,' said Virginia Woolf.

It is time to change that.

This won't sound like fun to those of you who are not keen on self-promotion. After all, we can all name men who seem to spend 55 per cent of their time on their own PR – and we don't want to be identified with them.

Why is doing your own PR so important?

According to research undertaken in 2009:

> There is a deep-rooted belief among women that if they do a good job they will be promoted, recognized and rewarded [. . .] [but] moving into leadership roles [. . .] takes more than doing things right.

It is not enough just to be good at your job – you need to make sure people know that you are. Women often ignore this because they believe that self-promotion is inappropriate. American marketing consultant Kelly Watson puts these detrimental beliefs into four categories. See if any of them ring alarm bells in your head.

- The Bitch Myth ('Self-promotion will make me look arrogant')
- The Princess Myth ('If I'm good enough, people will hear about it')
- The Friends and Family Myth ('Others should talk about my accomplishments, not me')
- The Martyr Myth ('You can't control what people think, anyway').

Which myth(s) do you subscribe to?

Melanie Healey, North America president, Procter & Gamble, when asked for her advice for younger women, said:

> [at] P&G, we often refer to a model we call PIE: focus on Performance (delivering the best results you can deliver); Image (building a strong and sustainable image, reputation and credibility, including strong integrity) and Exposure (ensuring you are getting the exposure needed to progress to the next level).

Notice that two of those three areas of advice concern effective PR – developing the right image, and getting the right exposure.

So, start by writing down a list of things that you want to be associated with and known for.

Excellent performance, of course, but what else?

Supportiveness?

Generosity?

Being an expert in a particular area?

Having excellent connections?

Overall, what message do you want to project about yourself?

Once you have honed the message, you have to deliver it. In a well-thought-out and carefully executed PR campaign, the distribution channels of the message are as important as the message itself.

Make sure the Internet works for you, not against you

In the second decade of the twenty-first century, the Internet is a powerful distribution channel for information.

What can people find out about you on the Internet?

Younger women reading this (and older ones!) may well have Facebook, LinkedIn, Twitter and other social media pages. Are these pages, and everything on them, consistent with the message that you would wish to portray about yourself?

Do your profiles include photographs or comment that might undermine the image that you would like to develop?

I find it astonishing that young people at college, who are competing in the harshest job market for generations and need to secure scarce internships along the way, often – deliberately – post pictures of themselves on the Internet in various stages of undress or inebriation.

And don't get me started on what some people tweet about!

LinkedIn

Make sure your LinkedIn profile is up to date and clearly represents the qualities that you would like to portray to potential employers. Remember, LinkedIn is your digital CV – your personal balance sheet for the Internet.

List all employment, major accomplishments, awards and characteristics that set you apart.

Do you speak four languages?

Do you write a blog followed by thousands?

Well, LinkedIn offers space to promote this (remember that 'third dimension' we talked about). Where possible, ask clients and former colleagues to provide recommendations. In an age increasingly dominated by the Internet, your online profile is as important as any PR can be.

Google alerts

To keep track of your online profile, set up a Google alert for yourself. If a friend posts an inappropriate photograph, ask them to take it down. If someone writes something that is untrue and disadvantageous, seek to get it amended or withdrawn. There is a limit to what you can manage to control, particularly as you become better known and more established in your career.

I remember the first time that someone posted something very unpleasant about Mrs Moneypenny on the Internet. I had got used to abusive comments posted at the end of articles I had written containing strong views, but unpleasant articles about me in particular represented a whole new dimension. I sought advice and was told not to bother setting the record straight because, unless it was libellous, it simply wasn't worth it. Instead, I set about making sure that positive coverage of Mrs Moneypenny increased instead, in order to have a better balance.

The most important distribution channel for the message about you is . . . you

You might think it is a bit girly to start talking about PR with some observations on appearance, but it is just as important as building an online profile. Trading in what I referred to earlier as 'erotic capital', a term coined by academic Catherine Hakim, goes beyond sexual attractiveness to include:

> charm and social skills, physical fitness and liveliness [. . .] skills in self-presentation, such as face-painting, hairstyles, clothing and all the other arts of self-adornment.

I am thinking more Michelle Obama than Jordan or Pamela Anderson.

Look at ambitious and successful men – they are never going to get a job just because they are incredibly handsome or attractive, but what they ensure, wittingly or unwittingly, is that they never lose the chance of advancement because they are badly groomed. By making sure that they are appropriately turned out and presented, they effectively remove appearance as a consideration.

It is a taller order for women to eliminate appearance as a factor in their career progression because there is no standard 'uniform', such as cropped hair, and a shirt and tie. But bear in mind that most people make up their minds about someone in the first thirty seconds. How you look, speak and engage with others – all these are critical to helping you get ahead.

Dress for success

I was once consulted by a young woman in a professional services firm who aspired to be made a partner. Despite working away at her role assiduously, going the extra mile, and having already taken on board all the suggestions in the previous chapters of this book, she had not been selected for advancement. She sat in front of me, bemoaning her fate and asking me what she could possibly do differently.

I suggested that perhaps one of the things she could do differently was dress like a partner in her firm. I asked her to describe the existing female partners to me.

How many of them, I asked, displayed as much cleavage as she did?

And how many of them wore the inappropriately bright colours she was wearing on the day she came to see me?

It pays to remember – clothes matter.

My colleague Vanessa Friedman at the *Financial Times* wrote a piece last year about looks mattering to female politicians. They matter, of course, to every ambitious woman – whether their aspirations are in politics, commerce or the not-for-profit arena. Vanessa reminded us that:

before any speech is even heard; before it has been decided who won or lost a debate; before votes are cast, judgements are made. Judgements based, primarily, on assumptions about how someone looks – starting with what they are wearing. *)*

This is true for men as much as for women.

Sort out your wardrobe – including shoes that you can actually walk in.

Find some role models.

What do they wear?

I am typing this beside a copy of the *FT* with a photo of Christine Lagarde, the head of the International Monetary Fund, who I have met on a few occasions. She is wearing a navy suit, cream top and discreet diamond jewellery – she looks elegant and professional.

You may prefer wacky clothes, and even see them as an opportunity to manifest your individuality, but I would suggest that from a very early age you should dress as though you expect to reach the top.

I bought my first Hermès scarf at twenty-six. I had worked out that the women I aspired to be like all had Hermès scarves. (I have since accumulated many more, and also a book, published by Hermès and given away in their stores on request, called *How to Wear Your Hermès Scarf*, which I thoroughly recommend for ambitious women!)

The best thing I ever did was go and ask for some help. I went to a store where I knew I liked the clothes, which were classic and businesslike, and asked for someone to help me. This saved time (she brought lots of clothes into one room for me to try on, which I did at the end of a working day) and money (by not buying the wrong thing). I now go regularly with one or two girlfriends, spending an hour or so in the store in the evening with a personal shopper.

Consider your wardrobe an important investment in your career. If purchased correctly, the return on your investment will far outshine the costs – and perhaps the heartache of throwing away that lime-green mini skirt.

Get the right haircut

If you think it is a regressive step to encourage ambitious women to worry about what they wear, you might not like the next piece of advice.

Hair also matters.

In 2001, Hillary Rodham Clinton was the speaker at Yale's 300th Commencement as Class Day. Dressed in a blue trouser suit, Hillary stood before a crowd of nearly 20,000 and talked about public service, children's issues and the global AIDS crisis.

But what is quoted most about that speech?

What do people remember?

The then senator and former First Lady told them, with a very serious tone:

the most important thing I have to say to you today is that hair matters. This is a life lesson my family did not teach me. Wellesley and Yale Law School failed to instil [it too]. Your hair will send significant messages to those around you [...] Pay attention to your hair, because everyone else will.

There is more to life than hair, but it's a good place to start sorting out how you present yourself.

Men have it so easy, don't they?

Some of them might worry about being follicly challenged, but maintaining what hair they do have is hardly taxing. We women have to worry about the cut, the colour, the style and, for those of us who appear in public from time to time, the need for a blow-dry.

I am told by well-placed sources that the late Diana, Princess of Wales, saw the hairdresser every morning. So too, apparently, does Anna Wintour, editor-in-chief of American *Vogue*.

Of course, women early in their career can't afford this. But they can put thought into what cut and colour they go for, so as to make the maintenance manageable. Maybe investing in that Brazilian blow-dry, if you have frizzy hair, is a better idea than a new dress. If you have the kind of hair that looks so much better when someone else has dried it, get it done before all important events, if you can.

I used to resent the time spent at the hairdresser, but it makes me feel so much more confident – and they have power sockets all the way through the salon, so I can keep on working. My real time-saving tip is to have the hairdresser come to you – but that is a luxury few of us can afford. A more economical suggestion is to always carry a hairbrush with you. Before presentations (and even walking into the morning meeting), pop into the washroom for two minutes and style your hair.

It's free – and it makes loads of difference to how people perceive you.

The final solution may be to date a hairdresser – as Julia Gillard, the Prime Minister of Australia, does. Or get your daughter to marry one. I recently met hair guru Frédéric Fekkai's mother-in-law.

At what point, I asked, when her daughter first brought Frédéric home, did she work out the net value of twenty years' free hairdressing, lock him in the house and book the church?

Because that is what I would have done!

Don't neglect the daily essentials

Vanessa Friedman included Hillary Clinton's comments on hair in her article, and also this observation.

Consider: before running for President of Brazil, Dilma Rousseff had her teeth and eyes done, lightened her hair and hired designer Alexandre Herchcovitch as a consultant – and during the election, no one blinked. How she looked mattered.

Yes, nails, eyebrows, any facial hair – all this needs to be addressed. I see it as maintenance, as a necessary investment in eliminating appearance as a reason for being held back.

Here is what I would recommend as the absolute day-to-day handbag essentials that every ambitious woman needs in order to keep her perpetually 9 a.m. fresh:

- concealer
- spare tights
- lipstick, and
- hairbrush.

Keep your focus on the message you are trying to present about yourself (both on- and offline), and make sure you look the part.

What next?

You've got to be visible to the right people

This is why the lessons of Chapter 2 are so important.

One woman director in the US Catalyst report on women board members said:

> present yourself in an environment where people can see you in action [...] they'll consider you as a candidate and they'll consider you way faster than if you knock on someone's door and give them your resume.

Such strategic networks are often broad (including fairly distant contacts who refer women for board seats), professional and community-based. Another woman director felt that even with the growth of executive search firms, most new board members are still referred through internal networks.

Develop yourself as a thought leader

Ask yourself two crucial questions.

Do you get to the places where you see the right people?

Are you even being invited to those places?

If the answer is no, one suggestion I would make is to develop yourself as a thought leader. It doesn't matter if you are at an early stage in your career – you can still make yourself an expert on a subject relevant to your chosen career, and then make sure everyone knows that you are. I am not suggesting boring people at dinner parties, but perhaps establishing your own blog, or writing articles for industry publications.

When I joined the company that I eventually bought, twelve years ago, I wondered how I was going to establish myself as a thought leader in my field. I found a trade magazine that covered the area and set myself the challenge of seeing if they would give me my own column. Eventually, they did – trade magazines are notoriously short of money, and I was offering to do this for free. I had enough of a track record (I had been writing the Mrs Moneypenny column for two years at the time) to prove to them that I could sustain it. Plus, I did a couple of dummies to reassure them that I would not be using the column simply as an opportunity to plug my firm.

For the next year, I wrote each month on the subjects I was trying to become known for.

A decade later, I am not sure I would bother.

Today I would just have designed a website, put a weekly comment piece on it, and populated the rest of the site with links to other relevant articles and news items available on the Internet. The important thing is to build a body of evidence, in writing, accessible by relevant others, that establishes you as an authority in your chosen area. Then you might be asked to speak at conferences, or contribute work to a journal.

I would encourage you to take thought leadership very seriously and think how best you can achieve it. If you are at an early stage of your career, I would encourage you to do some part-time study and publish papers along the way. As part of my own journey of self-promotion I studied for my PhD on a part-time basis (outside the USA it is quite common for PhDs to be awarded by research, rather than having a classroom component as a full-time academic programme) and so had the resources of the university and lots of potential co-authors to work with.

I presented my findings at academic conferences (it is very easy to find them and get on to the schedule). In 2008, I even joined the Academy of Management and got a paper accepted.

Going to the conference presented an opportunity to meet lots of interesting and relevant people – even in the departure lounge at Heathrow, where I found myself sitting close to a famous radio and TV personality. I had appeared on his show the previous year and had quite a long and jolly conversation with him, but you can be sure that when someone is wearing sunglasses in the departure lounge they are not in the market for unsolicited approaches.

Then, on board our flight, I came face to face with an Oscar-nominated screenwriter in the seat to my left. Unfortunately, his first words to me were to explain that he was going to put up the privacy screen.

What is the etiquette for privacy screens?

Should you ask the person next door if they mind you putting your screen up?

And what do you do if it turns out they do mind?

What if you are married to them?

But the screen went up, and I sat there worrying that I had developed body odour (or worse, halitosis), or that I maybe wasn't looking sufficiently glamorous or intellectual – unlikely, I know, but we should never rule these things out.

I examined my in-flight reading:

- *Financial Times*
- *The Economist*

▓ *Air Law* by Jeremy Pratt, and
▓ *The PowerBook* by Jeanette Winterson.

This tells you something else about doing your own PR – when you are going to be in public places reading books, make sure you are reading material that will position you correctly (see Chapter 7 to remind yourself why I carry a copy of the *FT* with me everywhere).

You just never know who you might run into.

Take control of your own PR within the workplace

This is something you must address, whether you are being well managed or not.

This doesn't mean ccing your boss on all your email to show how hard you are working. But I would encourage people at the earlier stages of their career to ask for formal monthly meetings with the people they report to. Don't position it as a 'showing off' opportunity – instead, position it as mentoring, or regular reviews. That means you will get one-on-one face time with your line manager each month, allowing you to run over the things you are pleased with having achieved in the previous four weeks.

We are all busy people and, if you are not careful, your boss may not see all of your achievements.

If this sounds a bit pushy, just watch what men do!

In a 2011 study of more than 100 senior women in financial services, many women felt that men were more visible to seniors.

Female bosses gave examples of male direct reports, who would find any excuse to come to their office and be seen. In contrast, they spoke about coaching their female employees to be more visible in the organization.

Communications consultants Steven Pearce Associates suggest that when putting yourself forward for an assignment, you should always have a handful of case studies up your sleeve that demonstrate your credentials by, in effect, saying: 'I've been there, done that, and added very specific value along the way.'

I recommend that you prepare a case study after each successful assignment you've completed. In a year's time, when you are looking to move departments or companies, you will remember specifically what you did to add value to the assignment. You should also look out for internal opportunities to move between departments, especially if you are in a large firm, to build your profile internally as well as gain experience.

Do more than your 'day job' – get involved in events, marketing, recruiting and community investment projects, corporate social responsibility or pro bono initiatives. Take every opportunity someone gives you, no matter how small it may seem at the time, or even if you feel you can't do it.

Keep key people updated on your achievements

Another key element of any PR campaign is the press release.

I am not suggesting that you send out press releases about yourself, but I do recommend that you write yearly to people who might wish to hear how you are getting on – and be achievement-oriented.

This is particularly true of people who might need to provide you with a reference in the future. Nothing is more annoying to your college tutor than to be asked for a reference for a student who graduated several years ago, only to find they have no idea what the student has been doing since that time.

Best practice for ambitious people is to select one person from each phase of your life as you leave it, and stay in touch with them for ever.

So, as you leave college, it will usually be your personal tutor, or a professor who knows you well. It might be your boss, or someone you have worked with closely, in every job that you have held. In the January of every year, write (or email) all of them and let them know how the last year has been for you professionally – and even personally, if you have had a major milestone (got married/had a baby).

Explain to the person you select as you finish each phase of your life why you would like to remain in contact – 'Do you mind if I stay in touch in case I ever need a reference in the future?'

Regular investment (annually is fine, more often can feel like stalking) in your referee networks is an important part of doing your own PR. If you have need of referees at a particular juncture in your life, and it is several months since you last sent your annual update, when you write and ask if they are happy to be a referee for you, add a few lines about what you are up to and why you are applying for that particular role.

There are also the natural information networks that you have access to: your class from high school, at college, at business school.

Are you in touch with them all?

This takes us back to the world of Facebook, as the Internet is such an important tool when it comes to staying in touch.

Are all the forums run by your former places of education up to date on what you are doing?

Finally, do not forget the strength and value, for your own PR, of the brand of your schools and college(s). Back in Chapter 1 I argued that you need to support those brands in order to invest in the balance sheet that is your own CV. They are also important opportunities for networks and doing your own PR.

Don't be put off by labels

It is true that in this world of asymmetric judgements (he is 'well padded', she is 'fat'; he is 'a bit of a ladies' man', she 'sleeps around', and so on), women who put themselves forward proactively can be harshly labelled.

Don't fall victim to the oft-reported 'double bind' where women either try too hard and are hectoring, or are too diffident and don't make it clear that they want to be in the game.

Daisy Goodwin, television producer and novelist, has lamented this problem.

Women in charge are characterized by pejorative adjectives such as "bitchy", "passive-aggressive", "stroppy", "hormonal", "ball-breaking" and, worst of all, "mad" – words that are never, ever applied to men [. . .] Women are "bossy" while men are "the boss" [. . .] The passion that is perceived as visionary in men is still too often dismissed as hysteria in women.

*

In this chapter, I have set out to instil in you the import-ance of doing your own PR. Although self-promotion is alien to many women, it is essential to advancing your career.

The received wisdom is that assertive women can seem harsh and self-interested unless they also express warmth. A woman who communicates in a highly com-petent but warm manner quells doubts simultaneously about her ability and her likeableness, and this approach can increase her influence.

So, make sure you spend 5 per cent of your time on your own PR, but do so with warmth, and humour. If you inject a bit of your own personality into it too, you will be able to support your career every bit as success-fully as men do.

At any stage of your career

Your CV is your principal selling document, so make sure your CV is up to date and that you can send it out at a moment's notice – even if just as background information for a speaking engagement.

Here are my top tips for a great CV.

Do:

- Put your name across the top and your contact details on the next line. Nothing annoys a prospective employer more than having to search through your CV to discover how to contact you.
- Keep it to one piece of A4 if at all possible. A CV is a factual record of your career, not a selling document. The reasons why you are highly suitable for a particular position should be outlined in a covering letter that accompanies the CV.
- Divide your CV into three: 'Education' (including professional qualifications such as ACA), 'Employment' and 'Additional Information'.
- Make sure that you account for every year – chronological gaps will be spotted and queried.

Don't:

- Head it up 'Curriculum Vitae' – it will be quite obvious what it is.
- List your 'interests' by using a single present participle. Thus 'skiing, travel, reading' are not going to impress. Hopefully you have a third dimension to

describe. If you do, list them together with how much you have achieved, or how committed you are. Thus 'run regularly with the Hampstead Harriers' or 'contribute monthly articles to the local community magazine' are better.

- Include your marital status or how many children you have – it is not relevant to your ability to do a job, and you can always volunteer the information at interview if you think it appropriate.
- Use a fancy typeface that no one can read. Arial or Times New Roman are fine.
- Get someone else to write it for you, except in draft. Employers like to see how you present yourself, not how someone else does it.

Finally, a word on 'personal statements' which many people put at the top of their CV. Personally (and I know not everyone will agree with me) I hate them. And I never read them. They are written by you, and they are a selling statement, so they have no currency. For example:

Mrs Moneypenny is a brilliant self-starter who owns and runs a successful business and writes regularly for an international newspaper. She would be an asset to any organization.

Any 'selling' other than the CV itself should be done in a covering letter – or by the headhunter who is putting you forward, if there is one.

CHAPTER 10

YOU CAN'T DO IT ALONE

There is no such sentence as, 'I can't do it.'

That is what I tell young women when I go and speak in schools and colleges. I am trying to raise their aspirations, instil confidence in them, and give them the same springboard that generations of men have had in the past.

Those of us who are past our university days also need to keep this in mind. It can be easy to forget as we are confronted with the challenges of day-to-day life at the office and at home.

Today, there really is no such sentence as, 'I can't do it,' for women. Keeping in mind the ten things discussed in this book, women really can reach the top – with one caveat. In order for, 'I can't do it,' to be a valid sentence, one word has to be added. Because the real sentence is, 'I can't do it *alone.*'

Birgit Neu, COO of corporate development at HSBC, depends on her team.

⟨ There are so many of them who are really dedicated and make the effort to give 110 per cent, even on things that may seem like thankless tasks – those people are the reason I get up every morning. ⟩

There is another way of looking at it too: 'Teamwork is so important that it's virtually impossible for you to reach the height of your capabilities, or make the money that you want, without becoming very good at it,' according to Brian Tracy, author of *The 100 Absolutely Unbreakable Laws of Business Success.*

The importance of a support team

Years ago, I used to be a contributing editor to a supplement produced by the UK's *Bazaar* magazine (previously called *Harpers & Queen*). The supplement was focused on businesswomen, and I remember vividly a story about Christian Rucker, the female founder and CEO of The White Company, and in particular the photograph we used to illustrate it. Christian had been an assistant health and beauty editor at a magazine when she had the idea of creating a company that sourced all kinds of lifestyle products for the home, and sold them by mail order – all in white. At the age of twenty-four she started The White Company.

Speaking in 2004, Christian said:

Juggling a business with four children is a roller-coaster. It's controlled chaos. But I think the key is to surround yourself with the right people. I didn't have children when I started the business [...] It's demanding, which is why I really need people I can trust around me; they are an essential part of making things work [...] It all falls apart very easily without them.

Christian then (and probably now) had an army of support in the form of a personal assistant, caterer, her mother, interior designer, Pilates instructor, hairdresser, managing director of The White Company, housekeeper, nanny and – last, but not least – her husband (who is managing director of mail-order clothing company Charles Tyrwhitt).

We had a photo taken of her with her support team, and the picture made the point very strongly – even more strongly than the list does in words. Just to get one woman to be able to function at her best at the helm of a company, it took ten people to support her on a daily basis.

Today, team Rucker will extend much further than those ten people. There will be all the staff of The White Company, all the suppliers, and all the customers. For any working mother to function on a daily basis might take ten people but, in order to deliver the results that will help you achieve your ambitions, you will need the help of many more – and many of them will never meet you personally. If The White Company was a publicly traded company, as many companies are, you would have to add the shareholders to the list of people who support Christian in her ambitions. And those who influence them – the stock analysts, the media, and so on.

Remember our discussion of the eleven female Chinese billionaires in Chapter 6? These women understand that they can't do it alone. As discussed in the *Financial Times*, with a combination of low-cost childcare and family support, Chinese women are able to work on average 71 hours per week.

Sheryl Sandberg, COO of Facebook, gave the 2011 Commencement Speech at Barnard College in New York City. She discussed the importance of choosing 'a life partner to share the responsibilities of the home'. Although women naturally bear the majority of household responsibilities, it is important that, in conjunction with other supporters, spouses are also team members.

I certainly don't say 'thank you' enough to Mr M.
So, here you are: Thank you! THANK YOU!

How to extend your support team at work

There may be careers where success is dependent on you
and you alone – but I can't think of any. Even the most
lonely lab scientist needs technicians. The most solitary
writer needs readers, publishers – and even competition
judges – to support their careers, if they are going to
achieve their ambitions.

You will notice I am extending the concept of 'teamwork' outside the usually understood description, far
beyond the small group of people that you interact with
on a daily basis at work. Really successful women recognize that they need legions of team members on their
side to succeed.

This brings us to the first rule of building a team that
supports you.

Regard everyone you meet as somebody with something to contribute

That is a very polite way of saying what all successful
women know: be careful whose heads you tread on, on
your way to the top, because they will be attached to the
backsides of those you need to kiss on the way back down.

These are not my values because I am such a marvel-
lous, inclusive person – they are my values because they
deliver results.

When asked by the *FT* in June 2010, 'What is your golden rule?' Barbara Stocking CBE, CEO of Oxfam GB since 2001, replied:

> That people are of equal value. So I don't change my style dealing with the shopkeeper in the village or the UN Secretary-General.

Employ the right people

The cornerstone of the success of the business I run are the people I have working with me. Ask any successful woman and she will tell you the same thing.

Julie Diem Le, thirty-four, was an eye surgeon before she began her business, Zoobug, producing safe sunglasses for children in 2006. The idea came to her when she couldn't find a pair of shades for her niece that were both safe and (crucially) cool. The company has come a long way since then: Julie Diem Le's glasses are now distributed in more than twenty-one countries, and she is busy working on a line of Olympics-themed eyewear in time for 2012. She has this single piece of advice for other people starting a business: 'Get good people round you.'

Whether you're running a small start-up company, or a well-established one with an army of staff, this rule applies regardless.

Ann Moore, former CEO of Time Inc., believes that the only difficult assignment in business is finding good people and putting them in the right job. 'That's the secret,' Ann said in her keynote speech at the Annual Wharton Women in Business Conference, 'and it's really pretty simple.'

Andrea Jung, CEO of cosmetics giant Avon, says that she spends at least 25 per cent of her time on talent development, planning and executing it.

❛ Talent is the number one priority for a CEO. You think it's about vision and strategy, but you have to get the right people first. ❜

Deanna Jurgens, vice-president of sales (US beverages) for Sam's Club, agrees.

❛ My greatest accomplishment over the past four years has been identifying, developing and promoting strong talent on our team. Your results are only as good as the people you have, and our team has been our greatest asset and true competitive advantage in this market. ❜

Good teams are essential to the success of any business leader – male or female. But they are particularly important for women, who already carry a large share of child and home care responsibilities.

Promote the right people

In May 2010, Ursula Burns became the first black woman to head a Fortune 500 company, as chair and CEO of Xerox (XRX). She had joined as an intern in 1980.

Ursula recalls her mentor saying to her:

❛ You're very smart, you've got the gift of the gab. But unless you could do every single job yourself, it'll be the end of you. In order to get things done, you need followership. Not people just following, but leading you to a place. You've got to abdicate the centre. ❜

I recently looked at the criteria that some professional services firms use to decide who, among their employees, will be promoted to the very top roles in the company. Here is a list that one firm has developed.

EXPERT
Acknowledged professional at industry level.
Develops and disseminates knowledge.

LEADER
Motivating, authoritative, driven, respected and followed.

BUSINESS-FOCUSED
Generates results, wins business for self, team and others.

VISIONARY
Looks and plans ahead, unravels issues, finds solutions and brings others into outcome.

ACKNOWLEDGED
Recognized by peers as an authority.

MENTOR
Good at spotting, training and nurturing talent.
Capable of tackling succession.

BRAND CHAMPION
Passionate – speaks/lives the whole ideal of the organization's culture.

STRATEGIC
Strongly focused on objectives of the whole business, not just in their own area.

And here are three others.

An accountancy firm	A management consultancy	An investment bank
Client relationships	Client contributions	Judgement
Applying technical expertise	People development	Ability to develop negotiations with clients
Commerciality	Knowledge contributions	Technical skills
Credibility and communication	Reputation building	Mentoring
Developing self and others	One firm behaviour	Coaching/ recruiting
Growing the business		Leadership
Innovation and change		
Judgement and decision-making		
Leadership		
Organization		

What is telling about these lists is how few items on any of them relate to human capital – i.e., to technical skills. Many of them relate to relationships with others – as developers of others (recruiting, coaching/training, mentoring), and as influencers of others (clients, industry peers, colleagues).

Win the support of others

You may say that your ambitions lie outside the professional services sector, and that will be true of many who read this book. But look back at those two lists above – they highlight the qualities of people at the top of, say, an engineering firm, or a soft drinks company.

So, how do you become good at enlisting and managing teams?

There are acres of management books on this subject, which I do not intend to duplicate – and, anyway, I am looking to provide advice specifically to women.

My most important suggestion, as mentioned earlier, is always to identify and acknowledge the contributions of others.

Women are usually good at this.

Don't rest on your laurels, though – just because you're female doesn't mean you're automatically going to be an award-winning team manager.

Be approachable and encouraging

There is a dark side to all this, I'm afraid.

According to the CEO of a large corporation (speaking anonymously):

‘ women can be absolutely terrible to each other. We're [women] great communicators but women can be so intimidating – there is no need to be. Try and be approachable. ’

She goes on to issue another warning. Building effective teams should not mean you are bound to them – or to your employer, for that matter – beyond what is useful to you.

❛ Women become a bit too loyal. Loyalty can compromise experience. ❜

Men may not make headlines for being catty towards team members, but they rarely show encouragement either. One exception is the editor of the *Financial Times*. He takes time to write personally and to commend the people who have done an especially good job for him, or who have penned a particularly good article or column. It takes time out of his busy day, but the effect is to win his team members' commitment and loyalty way beyond what any financial reward could achieve.

Do you say 'thank you' often enough?

Even to your peers?

Or your subordinates?

Or your seniors?

Cultivate self-awareness

Self-awareness is another cornerstone of team success. Know what you are good at – and what you are not so good at – and surround yourself with others whose strengths complement yours.

This is tougher than you think – you need to make sure you get credit for your success if you want to get ahead (see Chapter 9), so it can be hard to accept that you are not good at everything. Here, as with so many areas of success, self-confidence is critical.

It was only when I became proud of my abilities in certain areas that I felt able to admit to my failings in others. I was then able to enlist the help of others who were strong in the areas in which I was weak.

I was heavily influenced in the early days of leading my little company when I heard Jill Garrett, then managing director of Gallup in Europe, speak at an event for business leaders. She pointed out that you could spend a lot of resources (time/money) trying to make people better at the things they were bad at, or invest the same resources in what they were good at and make them totally brilliant.

Makgotso Letsitsi, director of risk advisory services at KPMG, says:

> you need to recognize where your strengths lie, and apply them effectively in your quest for success – rather than trying to emulate what you perceive to be the strengths of other people.

Jill also said something else that I found very interesting when I heard her speak all those years ago: if you do not measure what you value, you will end up valuing only those things you measure.

If the only thing that your company measures is how much money you bill, money will be the only thing that anyone will value.

After I heard Jill say that, I went back to the office, threw out my company's measurement system, and devised a new one to get people to acknowledge the contribution of others. That way, we made sure that we didn't become dominated by a sales culture – which would not have served our clients' best interests.

Olivia Garfield, BT group strategy director, believes in taking time to learn what motivates fellow team members in order to get the most out of them – and the most out of you.

❮ Know the person. The chance of motivating somebody to really work for you and to really give their best is negligible if you have never bothered to find out if they have got two kids, called Luke and Charlie, and they are aged four and six. You don't have to know loads about them. You don't have to become their friend. But you do have to have a sense of what's going on in their lives. [. . .] Once you understand the human side of people who work for you, you then get a sense of what motivates them. Just because cash motivates one, it does not motivate the next. The more senior we get, there is a risk we speak too much and don't listen enough. ❯

In getting to know others, be sure not to forget to keep learning your own strengths, weaknesses, motivations and ambitions. Once these are mutually communicated, expectations can be managed and a team will function more effectively and therefore more successfully – particularly if you have team members who challenge or even oppose you.

It's back-and-forth development. You're always in both roles, no matter what stage you're at in your career.

Play to your strengths

'I can't do it alone' is a slogan that is bandied about by football coaches, pop singers, voluntary organizations and Lord Kitchener ('Your country needs you' implies that your country can't do it alone). But it is an essential principle in playing to your strengths and getting ahead.

Don't get caught up in the old advice to work on your weaknesses. Instead, adopt these simple strategies.

- Hire someone who is good where you are weak.
- Delegate tasks that you don't enjoy to others who do enjoy those things.
- Automate the repetitious tasks.
- Contract out the chores that you are not great at doing.

No matter how hard you try, it is unlikely you will ever be more than average in areas where you do not have an aptitude. Always working on your weaknesses undermines your self-esteem, since you will focus mostly on your deficiencies.

Acknowledging your weaknesses, and dealing decisively with them, will put you ahead of men – who, being so competitive, are far less likely to own up to any weakness at all.

Early in your career, you won't have the opportunity or means to delegate. But you can be inventive – swap tasks with other people to maximize efficiency and play to your strengths.

For example, offer to do your friend's tax return in exchange for her stealthily baking a cake for your boyfriend's birthday.

Fewer than two in ten people spend the majority of their time playing to their strengths, according to Marcus Buckingham's seminal *Harvard Business Review* article 'What great managers do'. There are two implications here that women can use to their advantage.

▪ Firstly, acknowledge your own weaknesses, and make sure you can articulate how you address them. I am reminded of what Susan Gilchrist, the managing partner of Brunswick's USA business, said when her now husband, the historian Andrew Roberts, asked her on their first date if she could cook. 'No,' she said, 'but I can pay in restaurants.'

▪ Secondly, don't waste resources by trying to address people's weaknesses beyond what is needed for them to function at the most basic level. Remember this when you are in charge of a team yourself – instead, concentrate on investing in their strengths. This will get much faster results for your team than anything else.

Most countries in the world – and certainly all of the most important financial, military and intergovernmental institutions – are run not by a head of state, chief of staff, secretary-general or CEO alone, but rather by a team of ministers, advisers, deputies and assistants. This philosophy has created functioning liberal democracies, won military victories, channelled relief to developing countries, and boosted economies.

The same principle applies at any level, on any scale. You are as strong, and as effective, as the people you surround yourself with.

It is not for nothing that Hillary Clinton, US Secretary of State, has named her website 'Team Hillary Clinton'.

In professional sport, such as football and baseball, players who don't support their colleagues are seen as agitators and are often transferred. In business and in sports, team players are highly valued. 'People who work together will win, whether it be against complex football defences, or the problems of modern society,' said Vince Lombardi, an American football coach whose name is in the Pro Football Hall of Fame.

How to extend your support team at home

Working women, and especially working mothers, will need to extend their support team at home as much as at work.

Acknowledge and reward those who allow you to go out to work

One of the things that has worked well for me, for instance, is incentive pay.

The days of nannies are behind me now that Mr M. does the lion's share of the childcare, but I had help with childcare from 1989 to 2010 – a total of twenty-one years.

When I hired nannies, I always paid them six-month bonuses, one of which was timed to tie in with my own annual bonus. If they left during the six-month period, their bonus was not paid pro rata. I always said thank you, remembered them at birthdays and Christmas, and wrote them notes when they had done something particularly exceptional.

As Catherine May said (see Chapter 6), I think that domestic staff – nannies, housekeepers, drivers, cleaners, and so on – should have annual appraisals, just like any member of staff at work.

Put the time and effort into people and, in my experience, on the whole they are happy to put the time and effort into you.

State your priorities clearly

I also think that it is important to explain, to the people who report directly to you, what your biggest priorities are.

What *must* they deliver to you?

For every nanny I have hired, I have explained that if they don't come to work, I can't go to work, and that has serious ramifications for everything – including my ability to give them a secure and well-rewarded job.

I explain that unless they are dying of bubonic plague (or something equally catching), or have been in a car crash, I need them to come to work. Feeling a bit poorly does not count. If they are feeling poorly, come and sit on my sofa and watch TV soaps with a cup of chamomile tea, rather than stay at home.

Reliability is really, really important to me in my domestic help, and I explain that in some detail.

Accept that 'less than perfect' is good enough

Inability to delegate is something that holds many people back. This is true of both sexes, but especially of women.

We are brought up to believe that we have to be brilliant in so many areas – academia, career, girlfriend, lover, wife and mother – that we find it hard to see a job being done less well than we could do it ourselves.

However, if you only get through the tasks you can do yourself each day, you will never be able to achieve your ambitions.

Be prepared to accept tasks done to 80 per cent perfection, or even 75 per cent. Establish what is most important to you in the tasks that you delegate, and then explain that to the people who are assuming responsibility for them.

Micromanagement will always hold you back.

Call on other parents and family members

As many of you will know, the 'team' that gets a working mother to her desk extends way beyond hired help.

Knowing other parents at the school can prove essential when the nanny is sick, or on vacation. (Yes, I know, it should be illegal for nannies to get sick or go on vacation – but there you are, they do.)

Building that network of backup is vital.

One of my colleagues at work, when she decided to hit the accelerator pedal on her career, moved to a totally different part of London so that she could be nearer to her mother and sister, because she knew she would need backup childcare.

Be proactive in doing things for other people

Even if you do not have children, you will need a network of supporters – your 'team'.

What about the concierge in your apartment building?

Or the plumber who you trust with a key so that you don't have to stay home when the dishwasher breaks?

The best way to build a network is to do something for these people before it ever becomes necessary for them to do something for you. Christmas, for instance, should be a time to write a list of all those who have supported you – not just your friends and family – and send them a small gift and a note.

The best team members I ever 'recruited' on to team Moneypenny in the days when I worked in an investment bank were:

- the lady who ran the switchboard (because she always knew where everyone was, and how to find them), and
- the man who ran the in-house catering (because he would pull out all the stops when I needed him to).

Leading teams at work is the subject of many, much more scholarly pieces of work than this book claims to be (see the Useful Resources section in the back of the book). Participating in teams (agreeing your role, delivering your part, challenging and advising where necessary) is also well covered in the management press.

But women need to build teams, in the wider sense of the word – by which I mean 'supporters' – even more than men, because we do, and will, need more support if we are to manage to have families at the same time as pursuing our ambitions. And when you get to a later stage in your career – whether you have children or not – your parents may well start to need you more and more.

Successful women, as we have seen in earlier chapters,

cannot have it all, but they need to do it all, because women (much more than men) tend to be the carers for their family.

In order to be able to do it all, you need to be able to enlist the support of others. See Chapter 2 for advice on how to build a network, and Chapter 9 for how to do your own PR.

Both of these activities will help to build that wider 'team'.

If you are ambitious, you will be able to achieve just as much as any man – but, just like a man, you will have to make choices, make sacrifices, and make compromises. Knowing what they are, and why you are doing them, is more than half the battle.

The rest is just execution – which, for women, is much easier than you think.

Good luck! And let me know how you get on.

At any stage of your career

How well do you work in teams?

Get involved by working with others both inside and outside the office.

- At work, raise your hand to help out your colleagues with an extra project, or volunteer to be part of the organizing committee for recruiting events.
- Get involved in a non-profit venture outside work that allows you to work with other types of people.
- At home, delegate tasks among family members; consider hiring a team for household help, if the budget permits.
- If you have not yet chosen a spouse, consider a husband who will support you as a partner in the home.

At the start of your career

Volunteer for projects, office activities and non-profit work that gives you exposure to working in teams.

At a later stage in your career

Do:

- Learn to delegate work tasks to colleagues you trust.
- Assign chores you are not good at to your spouse, children – and home help, if budgets permit.

Don't:

- Try to do everything alone – remember, there is no such thing as a superwoman!

EPILOGUE

One more piece of careers advice.

A final word to all the ambitious women who will read this book. When you get to the top – and if you follow my advice, you will do so – remember to turn round and reach back to help the generation of women behind you.

As Madeleine Albright once said, 'There is a special place in hell for women who don't help other women.'

ACKNOWLEDGEMENTS

The dreadful economic climate of the last few years has had at least one fabulous outcome for me. The extremely obscure high school that I attended, originally founded for the daughters of clergy, went out of business and was taken over by a much more famous school down the road.

It is much better to have a famous school on your CV than an obscure one.

I am delighted to find myself, by default, an Old Girl of Roedean.

But it is a real Old Girl of Roedean, Anya Hart Dyke, who has helped me most with this book. She is an assiduous researcher who seemed to deal effortlessly with the chaos that resulted from her author having a full-time job, a TV series, and regular columns to write, as well as creating this book. I could not have done this without her.

And thanks, too, to Faye Wenman, who found her for me.

Jane Lunnon invited me to speak to the Prior's Field Girls Sixth Form several years ago. In desperation for a subject, I thought of sharing with them the ten things I wished I had known at seventeen. Thank you to the girls who listened to me, and all the girls who have heard me speak since. Your questions have helped shape this book.

Jessica Seldon gets a special mention for helping me start the research before she found herself a proper job, and Brynne Kennedy Herbert for coming in at the very end and providing a perspective from across the Atlantic.

Thanks also to my editor at Portfolio Penguin, Joel Rickett, for encouraging me, keeping me going – and finally, in desperation, setting deadlines. And my editor at Portfolio in the USA, Jillian Gray, for being brave enough to come and sit through my stand-up show despite having never met me before.

Jon and Veryan Nield helped me over the finishing line by taking me to their peaceful holiday home in Tuscany and providing food, childcare and proofreading all week. They truly were the best kind of team any ambitious woman could have – see Chapter 10.

Finally, Mr M., Cost Centres #1, #2 and #3, and all of my colleagues at work, who have to put up with me every day, deserve a big thank you. THANK YOU!

Last, but not least, the women whose comments and careers appear in these pages. Many of them are Girlfriends of mine, and many others have never met me or heard of me, in which case I probably need to practise more of what I say in Chapter 9.

Either way, thank you. You are all an inspiration. As are the dozens of women not mentioned; sadly, I had a word limit!

Notwithstanding all of this support and help, the opinions on these pages are mine.

NOTES

INTRODUCTION

page 6 **As leadership expert ... to blame.** 'Boardroom diversity is a must for firms, executives say'. 24 February 2011. BBC News Online. http://www.bbc.co.uk/news/business-12559189.

page 6 **In a global survey ... a company.** *Reinvent Opportunity: Looking Through a New Lens.* 4 March 2011 (released on International Women's Day to help fuel dialogue on key issues affecting working women). Dublin: Accenture.

CHAPTER 1: WHAT YOU KNOW

page 15 **The Institute ... of the women.** *Ambition and Gender at Work.* 2011. London: Institute of Leadership and Management.

page 16 **This gender difference ... afraid to go for it.** 'Women in business: The secrets of their success'. 30 July 2011. *Telegraph.*

page 16 **She is not the only one ... the relevant experience.** 'Boardroom diversity is a must for firms, executives say'. 24 February 2011. BBC News Online. http://www.bbc.co.uk/news/business.

page 22 **She got some skills ... current today.** 'Gail Kelly'. Melbourne Business School website. http://www.mbs.edu. Visited 9 August 2011.

page 23 **GMAC ... bonus of $17,565.** Leah Bourne. 'Is business school right for you?' 9 February 2011. Working Mother website. http://www.workingmother.com.

page 23 **The other reason that some people do an MBA ... and £55,000.** Sian Griffiths. 'Does an MBA come with such a cachet that it is worth giving up your job to enrol on one?' 13 March 2011. *Sunday Times.*

page 23 **As Tonya Olpin ... opportunities.** Leah Bourne. 'Is business school right for you?'

page 24 **Forté Foundation ... make an impact in your community.** 'Getting your MBA: Overview'. Forté Foundation website. http://www.fortefoundation.org. Visited 9 August 2011.

page 25 **According to the Association of MBAs ... students.** Widget Finn. 'Flexibility key for women'. 20 July 2010. *Guardian*.

page 25 **Mori Taheripour ... to my plate.** Leah Bourne. 'Is business school right for you?'

page 26 **Henrietta Royle ... great in later life.** 'It isn't just for men in suits in the City'. 7 April 2011. *Independent*.

page 26 **Rachel Killian ... the compromises.** Ibid.

CHAPTER 2: WHO YOU KNOW

page 47 **Whatever filter you use ... 'relationship capital'.** Sylvia Ann Hewlett. 'The real benefit of finding a sponsor'. 26 January 2011. *Harvard Business Review* blog website. http://blogs.hbr.org.

page 48 **Here are some top pointers ... and what about.** Neil Munz-Jones. 2010. *The Reluctant Networker: Giving You the Tools and Confidence to Give Networking a Go.* Blackminster: HotHive Books.

page 51 **Lynda Gratton ... on the importance of networks.** Lynda Gratton. 2011. *The Shift: The Future of Work is Already Here.* London: HarperCollins.

page 55 **A study of more than 100 senior women ... helped them.** *Past Perspectives; Future change. A Study into the Experiences of Senior Women in Financial Services.* 2011. London: Muika Leadership and Odgers Berndtson, p. 22.

page 55 **One book about female leadership ... workplace advancement.** Alice H. Eagly and Linda L. Carli. 2007. *Through the Labyrinth. The Truth about how Women Become Leaders.* Boston, MA: Harvard Business School Press, pp. 173–4.

page 55 **Internal politics exists ... 'managing up'.** Avivah Wittenberg-Cox and Alison Maitland. 2009. *Why Women Mean Business.* Chichester: Wiley, p. 242.

page 56 **Crystal Christmas-Watson ... training program.** Katherine Bowers. 'Secrets to climbing the career ladder'. 25 January 2011. Working Mother website. http://www.workingmother.com.

page 62 **Alison Platt ... and Bupa.** Rebecca Smithers. 'I'm a believer – how women can achieve managerial career success'. 26 February 2011. *Guardian*.

page 63 **I am all for using ... social attractiveness.** Catherine Hakim. 'Have you got erotic capital?' 24 March 2010. *Prospect Magazine*.

CHAPTER 3: IT IS NEVER TOO LATE

page 73 **Anna Mary Robertson Moses ... Vienna and Paris.** 'Grandma Moses is dead at 101: Primitive artist "just wore out"'. 14 December 1961. *New York Times.*

page 75 **The 2011 list ... range of medical conditions.** Hannah Prevett. '35 Women Under 35: A vision of enterprise'. 27 June 2011. *Management Today* website. http://www.managementtoday.co.uk.

page 79 **Someone who started even later ... twenty years of her life.** 'Obituaries – Mary Wesley'. 1 January 2003. *Telegraph.*

page 80 **According to a charity for older people ... no maximum!** 'Extreme growing up'. Age UK website. http://www.ageuk.org.uk. Visited 9 August 2011.

page 83 **Failure can feel like ... haze of shame.** Tania Kindersley and Sarah Vine. 2009. *Backwards in High Heels.* London: Fourth Estate, pp. 60–61.

page 83 **Carol Bartz, former CEO of Yahoo! ... how to garden.** Monique Talitenu and Jill Wolfson. 'An interview with Carol Bartz'. The Tech Museum website. http://www.thetech.org. Visited 9 August 2011.

page 86 **In 2006 ... collection of essays about ageing.** Nora Ephron. 2006. *I Feel Bad About My Neck.* New York, NY: Knopf.

page 86 **Jane Shilling ... on her own middle age.** Jane Shilling. 2011. *The Stranger in the Mirror.* London: Chatto & Windus.

page 86 **In the same year ... purpose in their lives.** Jill Shaw Ruddock. 2011. *The Second Half of Your Life.* London: Vermilion.

page 86 **The name Julia Child ... with her new husband.** Alex Prud'homme. 'Mastering the Art of Julia Child'. 20 August 2004. *New York Times.*

page 87 **Julia fell in love with French cuisine ... wrote to her sister-in-law.** Marilyn Mellowes. 'About Julia Child'. 15 June 2005. Public Broadcasting Service website. http://www.pbs.org.

page 87 **Although she may have identified ... until she was fifty-one.** 'In pursuit of dreams: Our next 5 question challenge'. Women at forty website. http://womenatforty.com. Visited 9 August 2011.

page 87 **A book that sets out ... waiting for ever.** Suzanne Doyle-Morris. 2009. *Beyond the Boys' Club.* London: Wit and Wisdom Press, pp. 51–2.

page 87 **Francesca Halsall ... silver medallist.** 'Profile of a Champion Swimmer'. Francesca Halsall website. http://www.francescahalsall. com. Visited 9 August 2011.

page 88 **In an interview ... real crack at it.** Donald McRae. 'Fran Halsall: "My only bad dreams are where I forget my goggles"'. 4 July 2011. *Guardian.*

page 90 **Globally, women consistently live longer ... 81.9 years of age.** 'Life expectancy'. 30 September 2010. Office for National Statistics website. http://www.statistics.gov.uk.

page 90 **In the US ... 80.9 years.** 'The World Factbook – United States'. 12 July 2011. Central Intelligence Agency website. https://www.cia.gov.

page 91 **Shonie White ... just change direction.** Rebecca McQuillan. 'Never too old to change career'. 3 January 2011. *Herald.*

page 92 **Catriona Welsby ... create a successful business.** Gina Bell. 'How does she do it? Interview with Catriona Welsby of the Women's Online Business Academy'. 3 November 2010. Institute for Aspiring Women in Business Online website. http://www.iawbo.com.

CHAPTER 4: JUST SAY NO

page 101 **Kevin Leman ... 'extreme pleasers'.** Kevin Leman. 2010. *Smart Women Know When to Say No.* Ada, MI: Revell.

page 102 **The issue we have as a gender ... welfare of others.** Linda Babcock and Sara Laschever. 2003. *Women Don't Ask: Negotiation and the Gender Divide.* Englewood Cliffs, NJ: Princeton University Press.

page 102 **Men with independent schemas ... protect them.** Susan E. Cross and Laura Madson. 1997. 'Models of the self: Self-construals and gender'. *Psychological Bulletin,* 122 (1), 5–37.

page 109 **Madonna press conference ... to eviction on the spot.** 'Reporter feels the wrath of Madonna's publicist'. 25 September 2010. *New York Post.*

page 111 **In a book about female negotiation ... on relationships.** Patricia Farrell. 2004. *How to Be Your Own Therapist: A Step-by-Step Guide to Taking Back Your Life.* Hightstown, NJ: McGraw-Hill Contemporary.

page 111 **There is also the problem of gender stereotypes ... being 'nice'.** Cordelia Fine. 2010. *Delusions of Gender: The Real Science Behind Sex Differences.* London: Icon Books Ltd.

CHAPTER 5: YOU CAN'T HAVE IT ALL . . .

page 126 **Back in 2007, Carol Bartz ... strain on all of us.** Monique Talitenu and Jill Wolfson. 'An interview with Carol Bartz'. The Tech Museum website. http://www.thetech.org. Visited 9 August 2011.

page 127 **Claire Vorster ... mountain to climb.** Claire Vorster. 'The real
secret to having it all'. 14 February 2011. Claire Vorster website.
http://clairevorster.com.

page 128 **Nicola wrote a book ... no one can.** Nicola Horlick. 1998. *Can
You Have it All?* London: Pan Books. Author quote on book cover.

page 128 **She has never managed to shake off ... UK fund manager, I can
be.** Daisy Garnett. 'The truth about female stereotypes'. 14 January
2007. *Guardian.*

page 129 **Helen Weir ... deal with as well.** James Moore. 'Helen Weir: From
Marmite on toast to a budget hotel, it's back to basics in high finance'.
12 January 2008. *Independent.*

page 134 **She has been described ... of her own label.** Britt Lintner.
'About'. Britt Lintner website. http://brittlintner.com. Visited April
2011.

page 134 **In late April 2011 ... it's time.** Britt Lintner. 'Britt's tip – a letter
to my 18-year-old self'. 23 April 2011. Britt Lintner website. http://
brittlintner.com.

page 135 **Here is what she wrote ... say 'yes'.** Britt Lintner. 'I'm hitting
the pause button'. 30 May 2011. Britt Lintner website. http://brittlint-
ner.com.

page 137 **A study of more than 100 senior women ... 'champions of
fatherhood'.** *Past Perspectives; Future change. A Study into the Experiences of Senior Women in Financial Services.* 2011. London: Muika
Leadership and Odgers Berndtson, p. 11.

page 138 **Nicola Horlick ... make priorities.** Daisy Garnett, 'The truth
about female stereotypes'.

page 138 **Carol Bartz ... work for a while.** Monique Talitenu and Jill
Wolfson, 'An interview with Carol Bartz'.

page 140 **According to Cordelia Fine ... recommended for hire.** Cordelia
Fine. 2010. *Delusions of Gender: The Real Science Behind Sex Differences.* London: Icon Books Ltd, p. 57.

page 141 **According to a book ... ambition yet further.** Sylvia Ann
Hewlett. 2007. *Off-Ramps and On-Ramps. Keeping Talented Women
on the Road to Success.* Boston, MA: Harvard Business School Press,
pp. 48–9.

page 142 **In the UK ... paternity leave.** Catherine Hakim. 2011. *Feminist
Myths and Magic Medicine.* London: Centre for Policy Studies, p. 9.

page 142 **In comparison ... maternity leave.** *Ambition and Gender at
Work.* 2010. London: Institute of Leadership and Management, p. 2.

page 142 **Laura Tenison ... so be it.** 'Laura Tenison: For the glass ceiling
to be shattered, there needs to be a revolution at home'. 14 August
2010. *Independent.*

page 142 **When you go on maternity leave ... a 'non-job'.** *Past Perspectives; Future Change*, p. 12.

page 143 **Sheryl Sandberg ... it won't seem worth it.** 'Sheryl Sandberg: Why we have too few women leaders'. December 2010. TED website. http://www.ted.com.

page 145 **More recently ... real challenges later on.** Sangeet Asiva-Kumar. 'Insight into an entrepreneur'. 13 May 2010. *Nottingham Economic Review* website. http://neronline.co.uk.

CHAPTER 6: . . . BUT YOU HAVE TO DO IT ALL

page 160 **Roberts is frequently approached ... don't ring my husband.** Laura Craik. 'London's supermum'. 2 June 2011. *Evening Standard*.

page 160 **According to the UK government's ... of all lone parents.** Household Labour Force Survey. 2010. Cited in Gender Equality Duty fact sheet. Government Equalities Office website. http://homeoffice. gov.uk/equalities.

page 160 **The authors of ... contributes to women's burden.** Alice H. Eagly and Linda L. Carli. 2007. *Through the Labyrinth. The Truth about how Women Become Leaders*. Boston, MA: Harvard Business School Press, pp. 50–51.

page 160 **On average, in the USA ... women's 2.1 hours.** Ibid.

page 161 **This gut feeling ... by any research.** University of Hertfordshire. 'First concrete evidence that women are better multitaskers than men'. 19 July 2010. *ScienceDaily* website. http://www.sciencedaily.com.

page 161 **In fact, there is a whole body ... damaging for performance.** David Glenn. 'Divided Attention'. 28 February 2010. *The Chronicle of Higher Education* website. http://chronicle.com.

page 164 **Miriam González Durántez ... balance it.** Christopher Hope. 'Nick Clegg "killing himself" trying to balance work and family'. 11 July 2011. *Telegraph*.

page 167 **Liz is a good example ... a 50:50 division.** Paula Szuchman and Jenny Anderson. 2011. *Spousonomics. Or how to maximize returns on the biggest investment of your life*. London: Transworld Publishers, pp. 14–20.

page 168 **Ann Moore ... That's just the way it is.** 'Nine business insights from Time CEO Ann Moore, plus the mix-and-match women'. 30 November 2005. Knowledge@Wharton website. http://knowledge. wharton.upenn.edu.

page 169 **Angela Braly ... it works really well.** Leah Bourne. 'Most powerful moms of 2010 in pictures'. 29 December 2010. Working Mother website. http://www.workingmother.com.

page 170 **The husband of chief executive . . . support his wife.** James Leith. 'It's a tough, man-sized job being a househusband'. 5 July 2011. *Telegraph*.

page 170 **When Angela Ahrendts . . . west of London.** David Prosser. 'Angela Ahrendts: Exactly the right material'. 28 May 2011. *Independent*.

page 170 **Patricia Woertz . . . They chose hers.** Jon Birger. 'Patricia Woertz, the Outsider'. 2 October 2006. *Fortune*.

page 170 **Helena Morrissey . . . pipeline of women.** Sian Griffiths. 'Top women need "him indoors"'. 3 July 2011. *Sunday Times*.

page 173 **Moreover, parenting pressures . . . less well-educated counterparts.** Alice H. Eagly and Linda L. Carli, *Through the Labyrinth*, pp. 52–4.

page 174 **Baroness Virginia Bottomley . . . domestic structures.** Virginia Bottomley. Speaking at gender diversity study launch. 21 March 2011. Hosted by Nomura, London.

page 174 **Jenny Knott . . . can't be superwoman.** Jenny Knott. Ibid.

page 175 **The authors . . . authority as mothers.** Tania Kindersley and Sarah Vine. 2009. *Backwards in High Heels*. London: Fourth Estate.

page 176 **According to a study by the Center for Work-Life Policy . . . comes to childcare.** Patti Waldmeir. 'Chinese dominate list of richest women'. 12 October 2010. *Financial Times*.

page 181 **This is what Klein calls . . . going to do it.** Ruth Klein. 2000. *Time Management Secrets for Working Women. Getting Organized to Get the Most Out of Each Day*. Naperville, IL: Sourcebooks Inc., pp. 41–9.

page 183 **Klein highly recommends . . . in kind, or otherwise.** Ibid.

page 184 **Theresa Ahlstrom . . . it will happen.** Katherine Bowers. 'Secrets to climbing the career ladder'. 25 January 2011. Working Mother website. http://www.workingmother.com.

CHAPTER 7: FINANCIAL LITERACY

page 191 **Take the example of Lady Gaga . . . can I become.** 'Lady Gaga studies performance footage to improve'. 30 May 2011. Star Pulse website. http://www.starpulse.com.

page 192 **She disclosed . . . million in debt.** 'Looking THIS wacky doesn't come cheap! Lady Gaga admits she went bankrupt after spending millions on tour costumes'. 31 May 2011. *Daily Mail*.

page 192 **In March 2001 . . . but Thailand.** 'eMasterCard launches inaugural Index of Financial Literacy in Asia/Pacific'. 7 March 2011. MasterCard Worldwide website. http://www.mastercard.com.

page 195 **Women need more money than men . . . in their lives.** 'My story: From minimum wage to millionaire mommy'. Millionaire Mommy Next Door website. http://millionairemommynextdoor.com. Visited 9 August 2011.

page 195 **Go out and buy a book ... My Cleverest Girlfriend.** Merryn Somerset Webb. 2007. *Love is Not Enough: The Smart Woman's Guide to Making (and Keeping) Money.* London: HarperPress.

page 195 **Economics Professor Annamaria Lusardi ... some of my options in life.** Annamaria Lusardi. 'Women and finance'. 1 April 2010. *International Business Times.*

page 196 **Financial literacy is very important ... plan for retirement.** Annamaria Lusardi, Olivia S. Mitchell and Vilsa Curto. 2010. 'Financial literacy among the young'. *Journal of Consumer Affairs,* 44 (2), 358–80.

page 197 **Fawcett Society ... lack financial literacy.** Rachel Shields. 'Debt is a feminist issue: Huge leap in bankruptcy among women'. 25 July 2010. *Independent.*

page 197 **What's more, financial advisers ... financial matters as men.** T. Siegel Bernard. 'Financial advice by women for women'. 23 April 2010. *New York Times.*

page 201 **When PepsiCo named ... female chief executive.** 'Women in business: The Pepsi challenge'. 17 August 2006. *Economist.*

page 202 **Her previous job was described as ... information technology.** 'About us: Members'. Business Roundtable website. http://businessroundtable.org. Visited 25 August 2011.

page 204 **Helen endorses the view ... great place to start.** 'One 2 One – Helen Weir FCMA, group finance director, Lloyds TSB'. November 2006. Financial Management – Chartered Institute of Management Accountants website. http://www.cimaglobal.com.

page 204 **She has also previously stressed ... all of these skills.** Heather McGregor. 'Routes to the top: Follow the money'. 6 October 2001. *Financial Times.*

page 205 **When her departure from Ahold was announced ... strong balance sheet.** 'Chief financial officer Kimberly Ross to leave Ahold'. 23 May 2011. Ahold website. http://www.ahold.com.

page 207 **The proportion of female members ... fell by 3 per cent.** *Key Facts and Trends in the Accountancy Profession.* June 2010. London: Financial Reporting Council.

CHAPTER 8: THE THIRD DIMENSION

page 215 **In April 2011 ... the future of art.** Royal Academy Schools Annual Dinner and Auction 2011. 9 March 2011. Reported on the Royal Academy website. http://www.royalacademy.org.uk.

page 216 **In an interview in December 2010 ... a bit more loudly.** 'More women makes business sense'. *Financial Times* report. 7 December 2010. YouTube.

page 217 **If the conversation grinds to a halt . . . interested in them first.** Charles M. Marcus. 'Eight ways to stand out from the crowd'. Self Growth website. http://www.selfgrowth.com.

page 218 **Barry Taylor . . . material of your own.** Sue Leonard. 'Stand out from the crowd'. 13 September 2009. *Sunday Times.*

page 223 **In the UK . . . it is more like 6 per cent.** Susan Vinnicombe, Ruth Sealy, Jacey Graham and Elena Doldor. 2010. *The Female* FTSE *Board Report. Opening up the Appointment Process.* Bedford: Cranfield University School of Management.

page 223 **In the USA . . . Bloomberg Rankings annual analysis.** Jeff Green. 'Women lose out on US boards as Europeans get quota help'. 16 June 2011. Bloomberg News website. http://www.bloomberg.com/news.

page 224 **Helena founded the 30% Club . . . to talk about it.** Vicki Owen. 'Funds boss steps up a challenge to put more women in the boardroom'. 20 February 2011. *Financial Mail* Women's Forum website. http://www.fmwf.com.

page 225 **There is a website that lists . . . to fill a government quota.** Board Watch website. http://www.boardsforum.co.uk/boardwatch.html.

page 225 **One book on this subject . . . to achieve.** Peninah Thomson and Jacey Graham with Tom Lloyd. 2008. *A Woman's Place is in the Boardroom.* Basingstoke: Palgrave Macmillan, p. 58.

page 225 **In the UK, the Davies Report . . . 25 per cent women by 2015.** Lord Davies. *Women on Boards.* 24 February 2011. London: Department for Business Innovation and Skills.

page 225 **The report calls on . . . achieving the objectives.** Ibid., p. 4.

page 226 **the FRC does acknowledge . . . female employees.** *Consultation Document: Gender Diversity on Boards.* May 2011. London: Financial Reporting Council, p. 3.

page 226 **Viviane Reding . . . 40 per cent by 2020.** Ibid., p. 4.

page 226 **A study by Corporate Women Directors International . . . leadership positions.** Sylvia Ann Hewlett. 'Women on boards: America is falling behind'. 4 May 2011. Bloomberg News website. http://www.bloomberg.com/news.

page 228 **As the sixteen-page . . . know you belong.** Women and Equality Unit. *Brighter Boards for a Brighter Future.* 2004. London: Department of Trade and Industry.

page 229 **In an interview with Oprah Winfrey . . . made them feel.** 'Maya Angelou on Oprah'. 14 August 2009. Dr Kashonia's blog website. http://www.kashonia.com.

CHAPTER 9: DOING YOUR OWN PR

page 239 **According to research . . . doing things right.** Avivah Wittenberg-Cox and Alison Maitland. 2009. *Why Women Mean Business*. Chichester: Wiley, p. 240.

page 239 **American marketing consultant Kelly Watson . . . what people think, anyway.** Kelly Watson, 'The four myths of self-promotion'. 29 June 2010. *Forbes Woman.*

page 240 **Melanie Healey . . . progress to the next level.** 'Melanie Healey'. 27 April 2009. Women Worth Watching website. http://www.women worthwatching.com.

page 243 **Trading in what . . . all the other arts of self-adornment.** Catherine Hakim. 'Have you got erotic capital?' 24 March 2010. *Prospect Magazine.*

page 244 **My colleague . . . are wearing.** Vanessa Friedman. 'Power dressers'. 18 February 2011. *Financial Times* Weekend Magazine.

page 246 **The then senator . . . everyone else will.** Ibid.

page 249 **One woman director . . . through internal networks.** Laura Jenner, Monica Dyer and Lilly Whitham. *2007 Catalyst Census of Women Board Directors of the FP500: Voices From the Boardroom.* 2008. New York, NY: Catalyst, pp. 23–4.

page 252 **In a 2011 study . . . in the organization.** *Past Perspectives; Future change. A Study into the Experiences of Senior Women in Financial Services.* 2011. London: Muika Leadership and Odgers Berndtson, p. 13.

page 253 **Communications consultants . . . feel you can't do it.** *Women in Professional Firms: Strategies for Success.* 2011. Bristol: Steven Pearce Associates.

page 255 **Don't fall victim to . . . in the game.** Peninah Thomson and Jacey Graham with Tom Lloyd. 2008. *A Woman's Place is in the Boardroom.* Basingstoke: Palgrave Macmillan, p. 51.

page 255 **Daisy Goodwin . . . hysteria in women.** Daisy Goodwin. 'We're too harsh on the bitchy boss'. 27 March 2011. *Sunday Times.*

page 256 **A woman who communicates . . . can increase her influence.** Alice H. Eagly and Linda L. Carli. 2007. *Through the Labyrinth. The Truth about how Women Become Leaders.* Boston, MA: Harvard Business School Press, p. 165.

CHAPTER 10: YOU CAN'T DO IT ALONE

page 261 **Birgit Neu . . . get up every morning.** 'Birgit Neu'. Britt Lintner website. http://brittlintner.com. Visited April 2011.

page 261 **There is another ... good at it.** Samantha Chang. 'Being a good team player can help your personal success'. Single Minded Women website. http://singlemindedwomen.com. Visited 9 August 2011.

page 262 **Christian Rucker ... started The White Company.** Emma Tobias. 'The whites and wrongs of going it alone'. 18 January 2003. *Independent.*

page 262 **Speaking in 2004 ... easily without them.** Carrie Jackson, 'So solid crew'. October 2004. *Harpers Business.*

page 263 **Chinese women ... work on average 71 hours per week.** Patti Waldmeir. 'Chinese dominate list of richest women'. 12 October 2010. *Financial Times.*

page 263 **Sheryl Sandberg ... responsibilities of the home.** Ken Auletta. 'A woman's place'. 11 July 1010. *New Yorker.*

page 265 **Barbara Stocking CBE ... Secretary-General.** Emma Jacobs. '20 questions: Barbara Stocking, Oxfam'. 17 June 2011. *Financial Times.*

page 265 **Julie Diem Le ... in time for 2012.** Hannah Prevett. '35 Women Under 35: A vision of enterprise'. 27 June 2011. *Management Today* website. http://www.managementtoday.co.uk.

page 265 **She has this single piece of advice ... good people round you.** Rachel Bridge. 'Boom or bust? Checking up on our three entrepreneurs'. 25 May 2008. *Sunday Times.*

page 265 **Ann Moore ... and it's really pretty simple.** 'Nine business insights from Time CEO Ann Moore, plus the mix-and-match women'. 30 November 2005. Knowledge@Wharton website. http://knowledge.wharton.upenn.edu.

page 266 **Andrea Jung ... get the right people first.** Del Jones. 'Avon's Andrea Jung: CEOs need to reinvent themselves'. 15 June 2009. *USA Today.*

page 266 **Deanna Jurgens ... advantage in this market.** 'The Complete Q&A's!'. 11 January 2010. *Celebrate Arkansas Magazine* website. http://celebratearkansas magazine.blogspot.com.

page 266 **Ursula recalls ... got to abdicate the centre.** Ursula Burns. 'A Conversation on Leadership'. 3 March 2011. MIT World website. http://mitworld.mit.edu.

page 271 **Makgotso Letsitsi ... other people.** 'KPMG'. Top Women in Business and Government website. http://www.businesswomen.co.za. Visited April 2011.

page 272 **Olivia Garfield ... don't listen enough.** 'Profile – Olivia Garfield: A winning strategy pays off for a woman on her way to the top'. 15 March 2011. *Yorkshire Post.*

page 273 **Fewer than two ... to their advantage.** M. Buckingham. 'What great managers do'. 1 March 2005. *Harvard Business Review.*

page 274 **It is not for nothing ... has named her website.** Team Hillary Clinton website. http://www.teamhillaryclinton.com. Visited 9 August 2011.

page 274 **In professional sport ... problems of modern society.** 'Famous quotes by Vince Lombardi'. Vince Lombardi website. http://www. vincelombardi.com. Visited 9 August 2011.

EPILOGUE

page 285 **As Madeleine Albright ... help other women.** Madeleine Albright. 13 July 2006. Keynote speech at 'Celebrating Inspiration' luncheon with WNBA's All-Decade Team.

USEFUL RESOURCES

BOOKS

▪ Babcock, L. & Laschever, S. 2008. *Why Women Don't Ask. The High Cost of Avoiding Negotiation – and Positive Strategies for Change.* New paperback edition. London: Piatkus Books. Very detailed book, making academic theory readable, on the ins and outs of why women don't always get what they want in the workplace.

▪ Doyle-Morris, S. 2009. *Beyond the Boys' Club.* London: Wit and Wisdom Press. Mostly for women working in traditionally male-dominated fields such as science and engineering, tutoring the reader on how to play the game to get ahead.

▪ Eagly, A. H. & Carli, L. L. 2007. *Through the Labyrinth. The Truth about how Women Become Leaders.* Boston, MA: Harvard Business School Press. Quite an academic book and particularly useful on confidence issues and the work–family balance.

▪ Fine, C. 2010. *Delusions of Gender: The Real Science Behind Sex Differences.* London: Icon Books Ltd. A fantastic insight into how boys and girls are socialized into masculine and feminine roles.

▪ Gratton, L. 2011. *The Shift: The Future of Work is Already Here.* London: HarperCollins. A useful and comprehensive book on the importance of networks.

▪ Hewlett, S. A. 2007. *Off-Ramps and On-Ramps. Keeping Talented Women on the Road to Success.* Boston, MA: Harvard Business School Press. Useful on the subject of how women's careers can suffer when children arrive, with advice for employers on attracting and retaining female staff.

▪ Kindersley, T. & Vine, S. 2009. *Backwards in High Heels.* London: Fourth Estate. A highly readable, amusing and energizing book, focusing on the multitude of challenges that women face in today's world.

▪ Klein, R. 2000. *Time Management Secrets for Working Women. Getting Organized to Get the Most Out of Each Day.* Naperville, IL:

Sourcebooks Inc. Very comprehensive, step-by-step guidelines on how to get more done in less time. Although there are some anecdotes, it is quite a dense 'how to' read.

■ Munz-Jones, N. 2010. *The Reluctant Networker. Giving You the Tools and Confidence to Give Networking a Go*. Blackminster: HotHive Books. Great on practical tips for networking.

■ Tarr-Whelan, L. 2009. *Women Lead the Way. Your Guide to Stepping Up to Leadership and Changing the World*. San Francisco, CA: Berrett-Koehler Publishers Inc. Good on deconstructing myths surrounding good leadership and the need for systemic change. Lots of advice on how to 'step up' to the mark.

■ Thomson, P., Graham, J. & Lloyd, T. 2008. *A Woman's Place is in the Boardroom*. Basingstoke: Palgrave Macmillan. Very detailed and useful insights into the realities and challenges of getting more women on to boards.

ARTICLES

■ Hewlett, S. A., Peraino, K., Sherbin, L. & Sumberg, K. 12 January 2011. 'The sponsor effect: Breaking through the last glass ceiling'. *Harvard Business Review*. The importance of sponsorship in getting ahead and why women are failing to establish these all-important relationships.

NEWS AND RESEARCH (GLOBAL)

■ Catalyst – http://www.catalyst.org.

■ ForbesWoman – http://www.forbes.com/forbeswoman.

■ Harvard Business Review – http://hbr.org.

■ Institute for Leadership and Management – http://www.i-l-m.com.

■ Prowess – http://www.prowess.org.uk.

■ School of Management, Cranfield University – http://www.som.cranfield.ac.uk.

NETWORKS, ADVICE AND RESOURCES (UK, EUROPE AND USA)

■ City Women – http://www.citywomen.org. A long-established, select-ive women-only club in the UK with around 200 members. It is for more senior women, promoting mutual support and stimulation to members, and fostering friendships among peers.

■ Every Woman – http://www.everywoman.com. An online resource for women in business and female entrepreneurs offering training, career advice and mentoring, with 40,000 members.

■ 100 Women in Hedge Funds – http://www.100womeninhedgefunds. org. Has a presence in both the UK and the USA. They raise money and invest in education, and you don't have to be in hedge funds to get involved.

■ Institute of Directors – http://www.iod.com. Provides support in all aspects of professional life from business information and advice to professional development services, for men and women at all stages of their career.

■ London Chamber of Commerce and Industry – http://www.london chamber.co.uk. Membership for London businesses opens up a huge resource of free essential business information, together with a busy events diary with great networking opportunities.

■ Managers and Directors – http://www.managersanddirectors.co.uk. A strategic global mentoring network established to support, advise and inspire senior executives in their function and performance, providing future development for men and women.

■ Sapphire Partners – http://www.sapphirepartners.co.uk. Do a lot of work putting women on to boards and into senior positions, many with flexible arrangements.

■ The Women in Business Network – http://www.wibn.co.uk. Has a membership of 1,100 women, made up of small groups across the UK. For women who own businesses and women in management pos-itions.

■ The Women's Business Clubs – http://www.thewomensbusinessclubs. com. Women-only, over 30,000 members across the UK. Runs clubs and events for women in business, at all stages in their career.

- The Women's Business Forum – http://www.thewomensbusiness forum.co.uk. Established in 2010, this Europe-wide network is for men and women at all stages of their career. It seeks to encourage current and upcoming business leaders to work together to achieve more balanced gender representation in business.

OTHER

- Finance Talking – http://www.financetalking.com. Specialists in financial training for non-financial people.